BELIEF

and your

INNER VOICE

BY

ANDY HOLLIGAN

Shield   Crest

© Copyright 2018 Andy Holligan

ISBN: 978-1-911090-87-8
Third Edition

A CIP catalogue record for this book
is available from the British Library

MMXVIII

Published by

ShieldCrest
Aylesbury, Buckinghamshire, HP18 0TF
England.

www.shieldcrest.co.uk

Contents

CHAPTER 1

WHERE DID THAT COME FROM?

E very one of us, whether we are aware of it or not talks silently to ourselves all the time. We carry around with us an inner voice, some of which is positive and some of which is negative. Some of it is beneficial and some is destructive. It is not an audible voice that we can hear, but more like a silent, internal dialogue that goes on all the time. This little voice is the result of our life-long programming and experiences, and we come to conclusions about certain things. Unfortunately, much of what we tell ourselves is negative and false. As a result, this leads to negative beliefs, a poor self image and negative results in our lives. On the other hand, positive self talk leads to positive beliefs, positive results and a good self image.

For example, if we are faced with a crisis or tough situation, we tell ourselves if we are capable or not. We tell ourselves if we've got what it takes, and whether we think we can handle it. This conclusion is usually based on previous experiences. If we have failed previously at something, we tell ourselves that we are not good at that particular thing. Whereas, if we have some degree of success in that area, we will have a certain amount of self confidence about facing the task and we will talk to ourselves positively. These thoughts will then be stored away in our subconscious mind, as data, for future reference. If and when a similar situation arises in the future, these thoughts will automatically come from our subconscious and pop into our conscious mind and we will remind ourselves whether we are capable or not.

For example, if a person has failed in business two or three times, they may come to the conclusion that they are not a good business person (negative self talk). The thought or belief "I am not a good business person" is then accepted and stored away in their subconscious mind. And suppose some time later they are invited to look at a business idea which is perfectly legitimate and has the potential to make really good money, it doesn't matter how good the idea is, they may very well be close-minded to it because their immediate thought is "I'm not a good business person, so play it safe". As a result of this close-mindedness they will miss every opportunity, because of their negative self talk and beliefs.

The real danger is 'accepting' it because not until you accept something does the subconscious act on it. In other words, when it is accepted by the conscious, it is made real by the subconscious. This thought or belief, if accepted will then colour and taint everything else we look at. But just because a person failed in business before, doesn't mean they are not capable of becoming a good business person. They have the potential, but it may just mean they need to make a few changes in order to become a good business person.

For example, it could have been a poor marketing strategy that caused them to fail. It could have been poor financial management or even greed which caused them to fail. It could have been a negative attitude towards other people or poor customer relations that caused them to fail. It could have been a hundred different reasons, but the truth is, your mistakes do not make you anything. You make mistakes, but they do not 'make you'. You may have failed but you are not a failure. Instead, you are a person with great potential who failed. There's a big difference. Therefore you still have the potential, and always will have, regardless of how many times you fail. It's just a matter of making the necessary changes, in order to get different results.

If a person who regards themselves as a failure in business, makes the necessary changes and becomes a good business person, then the inner self talk of "I'm not a good business person" must have been a lie, otherwise they would not have been able to change. In other words, you can, through positive action, conquer the negative inner voice. I've known people who were shy and introverted, become confident public speakers, as a result of changing their beliefs and changing what went into their minds. Although I must point out that this change involved practice and took place gradually, over a substantial period of time.

Initially these people lacked confidence and had a fear of speaking in public. They had attended seminars, listening to other people speak. Many of the comments that were made during the seminars were things such as "I could never do what he's doing!"

Yet, little did they know that in a few years time, they would be doing the exact same thing themselves. At this point, they did not believe in themselves, but they developed belief in themselves by changing what they read, what they listened to and by speaking only positive words. As a result, their inner voice also started to change from negative to positive. During this period of time, they were also taking opportunities to speak in public. This positive action of courage also affected their inner voice in a positive way. The gradual change in self talk would have gone from "I can't" to "I can, but not very well" to "I can".

The most dangerous part of negative thinking is believing or accepting something about yourself which isn't true. This is very destructive because as long as we believe it, then it's true for us, unless we change our beliefs. Until we start speaking positively to ourselves, it will limit us and cause us a lot of misery. If a negative belief or self concept is causing you to be miserable then it isn't the truth. Jesus said "You will know the truth and the truth will set you free" (John 8: 32) Therefore, if it limits you, its false.

Many people never discover the power of positive thinking, and spend their entire lives holding themselves back, because of false beliefs and self imposed limitations. Consequently they spend their lives in psychological prisons. They're not there physically, but they're there mentally. The mind will absorb anything if you repeat it often enough. For example, if you were to tell a child that they were stupid, (not that I recommend that) they would eventually start to believe that they were stupid. And with many of us, that is exactly what has happened. Although we might not necessarily tell ourselves that we are stupid, but we talk to ourselves in other negative ways, by saying that we can't do this and we can't do that. We say we are hopeless at this and hopeless at that. "It's just my luck!" and similar statements.

3

We might say we are only joking, but if we say it often enough we will eventually start to believe it and it will control where we end up in life. Remember the subconscious cannot distinguish between a joke and what you are serious about. It takes everything literally and acts on it. It's a proven psychological fact that the more you think about yourself in a certain way, the more you think about yourself in the same certain way. Unless of course, you choose to break the cycle, by telling yourself different things and taking control of your mind. The longer you have told yourself something, the more of a battle it will be to get the subconscious to change, but through repetition and persistence, it can be done. If you have told yourself for years that you are not a confident person, and you keep saying it, then you never will be confident because that is the direction you are programming your subconscious to go. If you want to become confident, you need to break the cycle and start saying that you are confident, (in the present tense). You need to bombard the subconscious with statements of "I am confident" (now) to override and correct your inner voice. What I am talking about here is using affirmations. We will get into this in more detail later on. But the change must take place mentally, before we see any outward change. Only then, do we become possibility thinkers instead of 'impossibility thinkers'.

The second step for the people who aspired to become public speakers was to take action. We spoke about how they started talking positively to themselves and changed what went into their minds but that alone isn't enough. This is only half the battle. Action is the only way to build self confidence and destroy fear. I'm sorry but there is no other way. This would be their very first time of speaking in public, even if it only meant standing up in front of an audience and saying their name. In a situation like this it is very normal and natural to experience fear, but the important thing is to face your fear no matter what. You cannot get rid of fear by trying to logic it out or think yourself out of it. Nor can you get rid of it by reading text books. Only by doing the thing you fear, can you get rid of fear.

Many of these people still performed badly on their first attempt, but that wasn't what was important. What was important was that they had taken that vital first step and that they had the courage to try. Because without that painful first step, there can be no further steps. May I just point out that when I first spoke in public, I have never felt so bad in my life. I knew I had performed very badly, in fact, so badly that I didn't want to do it again. But I forced myself to do it again, a few months later. I knew that if I didn't face my fear, the fear would control my life. And to my utter amazement, I had made a substantial improvement.

As tough as the first attempt was, there was no way of by-passing it. Only by doing it and going through it can we improve our self confidence and get to the next level. But the interesting thing which happens is that our inner voice changes from "I could never do what he's doing" to "I can do it. I may not be very good at it, but I can do it" Which means that the original inner voice must have been lying to us, through a faulty self conception. Yet we believe it until we prove it wrong by taking action. But suppose none of us had taken that first step? We would never know what we were capable of becoming and we would never develop any more of our potential. Psychologically, we could be stuck in that mode of thinking, possibly for the rest of our lives. Not only that but we would spend our whole lives believing a lie about ourselves, giving it power over us, as though it were true. Sadly, many people live their lives like this.

Each time you get up to speak in public, and face your fear, you gain a bit more self confidence and you improve each time. On each occasion, although we are probably not aware of it, our self image and inner voice is also changing. Ironically, some people who have the biggest fear of speaking in public, end up being the ones who can't stop talking. I once heard a motivational speaker get asked if he still got the butterflies when he spoke in public. He said "Yes, I still get them, but now I've learned to get them flying in formation". I've also known people who say that they now get a real buzz out of speaking in public, whereas before, they used to be stricken with terror. Over a certain period of time, the change in their inner voice would have gone something like this:

"I could never do what he's doing"
to:
"I can speak in public, but not very well"
to:
"I'm gradually improving at speaking in public"
to:
"I'm not great, but I'm getting better"
to:
"I enjoy speaking in public!"
to:
"I am a confident public speaker, I love doing it!"

Quite a change from telling yourself you couldn't do it! All because you changed what you told yourself and had the courage to try. Notice how the same human mind is willing to accept something which is the complete opposite of what it was previously told. The truth is, the subconscious doesn't care! It will accept anything if you repeat it often enough. It doesn't care if it makes us succeed or fail. It doesn't care if it makes us happy or unhappy. It doesn't care if it brings us pleasure or misery, life or destruction, wealth or poverty, it simply obeys. Isn't that awesome? That's the power you have at your disposal!

Have you ever heard of a child who was a compulsive liar and told so many lies that he eventually started to believe his own lies? That's because his subconscious mind had been bombarded with certain messages so often that it didn't know the difference between truth and falsehood. Eventually, through repetition the subconscious became 'convinced' that it was the truth.

When we first start speaking in public, we usually have little confidence but tremendous fear. But if we are courageous enough to take that first step, and keep practicing, then our fear and confidence levels will gradually start to change. The change usually goes something like this:

(Initial attempts)

FEAR

CONFIDENCE

After a period of time it looks like this:

FEAR

CONFIDENCE

Eventually it looks like this:

FEAR

CONFIDENCE

We all have a different set of beliefs or internal programmes which operate simultaneously, at a subconscious level. As previously mentioned, some are positive and some are negative. For example, we might tell ourselves things like:

- "I know I'm good at football but I'm hopeless at public speaking".
- "I am good at dealing with people but I'm hopeless with facts and figures".
- "I'm a kind and caring person but I lack confidence"
- "I'm a hard worker but I don't think I'll ever be rich"
- "I'm good at cooking but I'm hopeless at reverse parking"
- "I'm reasonably intelligent but I've got a terrible memory"

Now these are purely examples, but it demonstrates that we tell ourselves a mixture of both positive and negative things. Sadly, studies show that the vast majority of what we tell ourselves is negative. So the above examples are probably quite patronising, in that they look like a fairly balanced split between positive and negative. I have merely listed a few examples but each and every one of us probably has hundreds of different programmes operating simultaneously, relating to different areas. These programmes are all stored at a subconscious level because our conscious minds can only think one thought at a time and would be unable to cope. So God has endowed us with an automatic part to our mind, called the subconscious, which does all of these things for us.

Not only is this where all our programming is stored, it also controls about 90% of all our physical bodily functions. For example, you do not have to think about making your heart beat or remember to digest your food. You don't have to think about which muscles to use when you are running along the road. You don't have to think about healing a cut on your skin or re-member to breathe. You don't have to remember to blink. It is all done automatically by your subconscious mind. The sub-conscious is also where our beliefs are stored and our emotions come from. Therefore it is no surprise that the subconscious is far more powerful than our conscious minds.

If you think about the person who believed that they were not a good business person, that thought, or belief was stored away in their subconscious. Although it was part of their belief system, or internal dialogue, there was no need for them to be consciously thinking about it. In fact, they were probably so busy getting on with their lives that that was the last thing they were thinking about. But it was still operating and controlling their behaviour nevertheless, even if they didn't realise it.

This inner voice would have the effect of colouring and tainting all future opportunities and therefore affecting deci-sions. So when an opportunity presented itself to look at a business idea, the thought "I'm not a good business person" immediately popped into their conscious mind from the sub-conscious. This is the principle of autosuggestion, which means that whatever is 'impressed' upon the mind, will eventually be 'expressed' in one way or another. Basically speaking, what we put in, we get back out. Our subconscious is our obedient servant, just waiting to give information back to us, whenever it is required. But it can only give back what has gone in.

But the one big advantage we as humans have, is that by changing what we tell ourselves, we can change how our sub-conscious performs. And we can change it at any given point. For example, the person who comes to the conclusion that they are not a good business person, could just as easily tell them-selves that they are great business person. They may have failed in business previously but instead of telling themselves they are a failure in business, they could tell themselves "I may have failed two or three times, but I know I have the potential to become great. I will do whatever it takes until I become a great business person" And this self-concept could have been stored by their subconscious instead. Thus, the subconscious would go in a different direction.

Different programming will always end up producing different results. The difference in programming (or inner voice) might seem apparently small, but the long term difference can be huge. Similar to the ship leaving harbour which is only one degree off course, it might not seem like a large amount initially, but once it has sailed for hundreds of miles, the difference in results is enormous. So it is with our words.

So if this persons programming was wrong on this occasion, how many other programmes do they have which are also wrong? This is a question that we all need to ask ourselves. As you read through this book, you will be shown how you can take control of your life, by changing your words. Your words then have the power to affect your beliefs, which can change the course of your life.

WHATEVER IS IMPRESSED WILL BE EXPRESSED

The subconscious picks up far more than we are consciously aware of. Think about a time when you have been driving on the motorway and away in the distance you can see a truck. Although it is too far away to read the writing on the side of it, you can still make out the colour and the basic shape of the logo. Automatically, the company name pops into your conscious mind from the subconscious, even although it is too far away to read. Where did that come from? How did you know that?

Obviously that thought must have been stored away in your subconscious, in order for that process to happen. So how did it get there, you might ask? Those trucks aren't important to me, and I certainly don't remember paying attention to them, trying to remember the company name, you might be saying. Well the answer is that you don't necessarily need to try, in order for something to be absorbed by your subconscious. The subconscious absorbs things far more effectively 'without' effort. Therefore we can be absorbing things all around us (subconsciously) without knowing we are absorbing them. 'Trying too hard' to absorb something can actually have the opposite effect because the anxiety we experience can block the information getting to our subconscious.

But the reason the company name was imbedded in your subconscious mind is that you have probably seen those trucks hundreds of times when they were up close, only you weren't consciously paying attention. But your subconscious took it in. It doesn't matter if you were paying attention or not and it doesn't matter if you tried to remember it or not. The subconscious takes in far more than our conscious minds could ever notice. So think about it, if something can make an impression on your subconscious mind without even trying, how much more of an impression can we make if we consciously decide to control what goes into our minds? That should be a revelation to all of us!

The subconscious doesn't care if something is important or not, it simply takes in everything which reaches it through the five senses. It never sleeps and is on the job 24 hours a day. I'm sure we can all recall a time when we couldn't get a particular piece of music out of our heads. Obviously this piece of music had to first make an impression upon our subconscious mind before it could be given back to us in the form of autosuggestion. We may not even remember hearing the piece of music because it wasn't important to us or because we weren't paying attention, but our subconscious absorbed it.

WE MAKE CONNECTIONS

Our subconscious is constantly trying to make sense out of all the input it receives by associating things with other things and putting them in order. For example, we may associate a certain smell with a certain place or a certain piece of music with a certain person. To illustrate this point, there was the story of the toddler who started school, and every day they would take with them their brand new leather school bag. Inside the bag, there was a very strong smell of leather. Unfortunately, the child had a hard time starting school and would often cry. But because they took their leather bag with them every day to school, their subconscious began to associate the smell of leather with school (something they dreaded) As a result, the smell alone could trigger painful and unpleasant memories, even if they were no-where near school. In fact, because they were at school for several years with this particular bag, the psychological connection between the smell of leather and school was firmly embedded in their subconscious mind. To the extent that many years later when this person had become an adult and was earning a living, if they simply smelled the inside of a new leather school bag, painful memories buried deep in their subconscious would come flooding back to their conscious minds and tears would often come to their eyes

The way the subconscious mind works is, when it stores or records an event in our memory, the emotions that were experienced at that particular time, also get stored with it. So that even if many years have passed by, if something triggers a memory of something, the emotions that accompanied that particular event also come out. Notice how, although the subconscious had made a powerful connection between the smell of leather and being at school, at no time was any conscious effort made to make this connection. It all happened automatically by the workings of the subconscious mind.

We may come across a person we have not seen for years, yet instantly we have either a positive or negative feeling towards that person. We may not realise why, but these emotions are based on our previous dealings with that person, or whatever information we have stored about that person. We may not remember what that experience was, but our subconscious has remembered it, and these feelings are re-lived, almost as if it were happening again. It is by making these connections that our subconscious gives us what some people call a 'gut feeling'. Our subconscious has taken in such an enormous amount of information in our lives, relating to so many different things, that it tries to communicate this to us by giving us hunches and feelings. I personally have never known a gut feeling to be wrong.

I remember one time when I was in my car, driving round a roundabout and had to make a snap decision. There was a choice of two different exits. Both lead to the same destination but one was a more direct route and the other was more of a scenic route. I had to decide quickly which one to take. I had a very strong urge to take the scenic route but didn't know why. But from a logical point of view, because I was running a bit late, I thought I should take the more direct route. I ignored the hunch and took the direct route. I got a few hundred yards along the road and suddenly there were signs saying "Roadworks" There were traffic lights and a massive queue of traffic which was hardly moving. The road was so narrow that you couldn't turn around and go back because of the traffic coming the other way. You just had to sit in it and wait. I realised right there and then that my hunch had been right but it was too late. Why didn't I listen to it? Because I thought I knew best. I thought my conscious mind knew more than my subconscious but it didn't. The lesson I learned from that is when logic is in conflict with a hunch or a gut feeling, go with your gut feeling, even if you don't understand why. It knows more than you do. I don't know why it does but it does.

When we meet a person for the first time, the feeling we have about them has a lot to do with subconscious communication, which is unspoken. A sixth sense if you like. Things such as eye contact, facial expression, body language and the 'vibes' are all contributing factors.

We may not know why we get a certain feeling about a particular person but we do. What our subconscious is really saying to us is, "Based on all your previous experiences since the day you were born, and based on every bit of information recorded through the five senses regarding this particular person or situation, I have arrived at the conclusion that ....", and our subconscious then proceeds to give us a hunch or feeling about that person or situation. This whole process takes place in a fraction of a second. That's why it's so important to make a good first impression, because we only get one chance to make a first impression.

Studies show that when we meet someone for the first time, within the first 30 seconds they have pretty well made their minds up about us. That's why it's so important to make a good first impression, especially if we have an appointment with someone. Because everything else could depend on that initial meeting. For example, if you had an appointment with someone to show them a business opportunity, you would probably want to stack everything in your favour. First of all, you would probably wear a suit and tie. You would probably make sure your hair was tidy and your shoes were shined and that they see you in the best possible light. In other words, you would want to give a professional appearance. Why? Because subconsciously, people associate business dress with professionalism. But supposing you showed up wearing blue jeans and a football top? How would they perceive you then? You could be showing them the exact same opportunity but their perception of you and the impression you make is completely different because of the way you are dressed. They might not even take you seriously because subconsciously we don't associate blue jeans and football tops with professionalism. So we need to be constantly aware of the image we are projecting.

It has been said that "everything about you, says something about you", which is absolutely true. For example, your hand-shake, and your tone of voice says something about your self confidence. Your facial expression says something about what's going on in your mind. The way you eat says something about your manners. The kind of music you listen to says something about you. The words you use says something about your atti-tude. The kind of people we associate with are usually a reflec-tion of ourselves. These are just a few examples of how we are constantly telling on ourselves, and it will affect how people perceive us.

HUNCHES AND AUTOSUGGESTION

A hunch is slightly different from our inner voice, in that a hunch is more like a feeling we get (or a sixth sense), whereas our inner voice is the inner dialogue we have with ourselves. There is a fine line between the two. Although I've never known a hunch or a gut feeling to be wrong, sometimes our inner voice can be wrong if we believe negative things about ourselves.

Some people have different beliefs regarding where hunches come from. They certainly seem to be from an intelligence greater than ours. As our subconscious is all-wise, and knows things that our conscious mind does not, some may argue that it is the work of our subconscious mind. Others may argue that hunches come directly from God. But whatever your beliefs, we need to remember that although our subconscious is extremely powerful, God is all-powerful. After all, He created our subconscious mind. But our inner voice can sometimes be faulty, so we need to become aware of what we are telling ourselves. The general rule of thumb is that if our inner voice is negative or self defeating, it is false. God didn't create us to fail or to be miserable; He created us to succeed and to be happy. So any kind of self talk which involves talking negatively to ourselves, needs to be changed.

Consider the example of the person who came to the conclusion that they were not a good business person. Here we can see an example of someone who has programmed their subconscious to work against them, by impressing upon it false and negative information. False, because everyone has the potential to be great, therefore it isn't the truth. Remember, autosuggestion is based on the principle that whatever is impressed upon the mind, will eventually be expressed in actual physical reality. Therefore, when a business opportunity comes along, they are automatically close-minded to it. The thought "I'm not a good business person" suddenly flashes into their conscious mind from their subconscious. This is what was 'expressed', as a result of what had been 'impressed'. In other words, they subconsciously 'made sure' they were not going to be a good business person, by shutting off any opportunities that might enable them to be successful and contradict their beliefs. Thus, the false belief would continue to be 'proved right'.

That is the 'job' of the subconscious ; to make sure that what we believe comes true. When something is accepted by the conscious, it is 'made real' by the subconscious. But the reason it had been impressed in the first place is because that's what they had decided to tell themselves. They had reinforced the belief, over a substantial period of time, through repetition. The key to making an impression upon the subconscious is repetition. The more frequent and repetitive something is, the deeper an impression it will make. Once a deep impression is made, the more reluctant the subconscious is to change. Only by knowing how the mind works and putting certain principles into practice, can we get the subconscious to accept new, or contradictory programming. More about this later.

The best way to learn anything is by spaced repetition. For example, we might take driving lessons or go to a class to learn martial arts twice a week. Eventually, through repetition, we will learn what to do until it becomes second nature (subconscious) In my opinion, the nights off in between those lessons is just as important as the actual time spent learning. That's why I don't believe in courses (in anything) which cram everything you might normally learn over a period of months, into one weekend. Because the mind doesn't work that way. All that will happen is you will experience 'information overload'. The mind can only take in so much, in one go. That is, it can only take in so much, without a break, before it switches off. Don't get me wrong, the mind can take in an unlimited amount of information, but it needs spaced intervals, to absorb what it has learned.

Emotion is another powerful factor in making a deep impression upon the subconscious mind. The stronger the emotion, in relation to a particular event or experience, the more of an impression it will make. That's why we have certain memories which we will never forget, and that goes for good and bad. It doesn't matter whether the emotion was positive or negative, it only matters if it was a strong emotion, in order for it to be remembered. Have you ever wondered where some of the thoughts come from that are in our heads? Take for example the story of a young girl who was criticised and told to be quiet, every time she sang a song.

She had a cruel stepmother who was constantly nagging at her and putting her down. Ever since she was a little girl, she had loved to sing, but as soon as she started to sing, her stepmother would scold her and tell her to be quiet, often ridiculing her at the same time. This went on for many years until eventually the girl became withdrawn and introverted. It had adversely affected her self-image. The criticism from her stepmother had made such a deep impression on her, that even before she opened her mouth to start singing, she could almost hear her stepmother shouting at her. She could 'hear' the cutting remarks and the criticism, before it actually happened. She now expected it. Her subconscious had made such a connection between singing and being criticised, that any time she felt like singing, words such as "Will you be quiet!" immediately entered her mind, even before she had been told off. Her stepmother's voice had made a deep impression upon her mind and it was now being given back to her, in the form of auto-suggestion. What had been impressed was now being expressed in her life.

Eventually after many years, she became a young woman and no longer lived with her cruel stepmother, but psychologically, the criticism had left its mark. Although she was now free to sing as much as she wanted, without being criticised, she couldn't get her stepmothers voice out of her head, even although she hadn't seen her for many years. Every time she sang a song, even if no-one else was there, mentally she could still hear her stepmother ridiculing her and telling her to be quiet. Logically, it no longer made sense. She felt as though she was still being criticised (and mentally she was) although, in reality she was not. Her subconscious had been programmed to operate this way for years and it was now haunting her.

Only by re-programming her mind, and speaking positive words was she able to gradually regain control of her mind and rid herself of damaging and destructive programming. It took many years before the voice completely disappeared from her mind because it had been programmed in for such a long period of time. But you cannot simply 'get something out of the mind' because the mind is never blank and we are always thinking something. It can only be replaced. Similar to covering over an old coat of paint with the new. Whatever we allow in will eventually replace the old.

Finally, after several years, her stepmothers voice began to fade from her mind. But one of the reasons it eventually disappeared was because there was no more input. In other words, her mind had been 'starved' of that particular criticism and 'fed' with positive instead. Whatever is starved will eventually die and whatever is fed will live. Simliar to the principle of water in a bath tub. If you stop putting cold water in and add only hot water, eventually the water will be extremely hot, because it has been starved of cold water. But if you stop putting hot water in and add only cold water, eventually the water will be very cold. In other words, whatever is being 'fed in' will eventually dominate and replace the other.

In the case of that girl, the criticism from her stepmother was no longer being fed into her mind but she began feeding positive into her mind instead. Eventually the criticism died because it was no longer being fed in. Instead, it was gradually replaced by the positive. In the same way, if we stop feeding negative into our minds, we will become more positive. It's the law of 'cause and effect' in action. The input is the cause and our state of mind is the effect.

It was many years before she could sing and be completely free from hearing her stepmothers voice, but through persistence and allowing only positive into her mind, she was able to overcome and replace it. She realised that if she had negative programming in that particular area of her life, how many other areas might also need to be corrected?

Obviously that was a negative example of autosuggestion which was caused by another person, but how many other self defeating programmes do we have which are operating right now which are self inflicted? Sometimes we beat ourselves up more than other people do. Sometimes we are our own worst critic. The principle of auto-suggestion is neutral and will work just as effectively in our favour as it will against us. But we must take control by telling ourselves what we want, instead of what we don't want and by controlling what we allow into our minds.

THE MAN WHO PROGRAMMED HIMSELF TO GET ANGRY

Some people unknowingly programme their subconscious minds to work against them. Through sheer ignorance of how the mind works, they programme themselves with negative emotions, and programme themselves to fail. As a result, they programme themselves to be unhappy because happiness cannot co-exist alongside negative emotions. The subconscious doesn't care if we succeed or fail because unlike the conscious mind, it has no reasoning of its own and cannot make decisions. But it does respond emotionally to our conscious mind. That is, it responds to every word, thought, deed and action with corresponding emotions. For example if we do something we believe is wrong, we will experience guilt and unhappiness. If we do a good deed for someone, we will experience happiness and pleasure. These are just two examples of many potential emotional responses.

The conscious provides for the subconscious by providing it with information but ironically the subconscious rules over the conscious because it is the far more powerful of the two. This may sound like a paradox, but when I say 'rules over it' I am referring to the emotions. Our emotions are so powerful that no amount of conscious thinking will ever change an emotion. In a sense, the subconscious, largely controls our mental state because it saturates our consciousness with emotions. Our emotions will always dominate our thinking. The only thing we can control is whether they are positive or negative. Therefore, by controlling our behaviour, we can indirectly control our emotions to a large degree.

Take for example the man who programmed himself to get angry every time he saw cars parked illegally. Every time he went out in his car, or even if he was walking, he would always seem to notice people with their cars parked illegally. When he was out with friends or relatives, he would yell to them "They shouldn't be parked there! That really annoys me!" and as a result, it did annoy him. He became unhappy.

His friends and relatives didn't seem to notice, let alone get angry, but he always did. Many times during the course of daily conversation with other people, he would bring this subject up and tell them how much it annoyed him. Until one day he realised how miserable he was making himself and decided to change his attitude. Not only was he making himself miserable but he realised that constantly talking about it or getting angry wasn't going to change anything, so what was the point? So from then on he decided that unless it was absolutely necessary, he would say nothing. He began to feel happier.

He also realised that the reason he was getting so angry is because he was programming to his subconscious to get angry, by saying "That really annoys me!" You cannot experience happiness if you are telling your subconscious to get annoyed. Words are very powerful and create emotions which will either be positive or negative. Whatever we continually focus on, we also programme our brains to look out for. This is usually done unknowingly. Part of our brain called the Reticular Activating System, controls our ability to direct attention towards specific areas of our conscious awareness. We then start noticing things automatically, without even trying.

Each time the man focused on illegally parked cars, not only was he creating an emotional response but he was also programming his brain to be on the lookout for them. The message his subconscious mind gets is "He keeps on talking about it so it must be important to him" and therefore he starts to notice illegally parked cars everywhere. But when he decides not to talk about it anymore, his subconscious stops receiving these messages and therefore stops drawing his conscious awareness to them. It's not that illegally parked cars are no longer there. They are still there but because they are no longer important to him, he doesn't 'see them'.

Our words are extremely powerful and creative. What we say is what we get. Negative words limit us and cause us to fail, while positive words free us and destroy limitations. One common example of limiting self talk is when people say "I can't afford it" Never say you can't afford it, or you never will be able to afford it. Is it any surprise when people who say "I can't afford it," regularly find themselves in financial difficulty? Not surprising at all really because that's the command they have given their subconscious. Through ignorance of how the mind works, they have programmed themselves to be broke.

Even if you feel that it's true and you really can't afford it, refuse to say it. Instead, tell yourself what you want. For example, you could say "I'll find a way to afford it" or "I'll need to raise some capital" indicating to your subconscious that it is possible to get out of this mess and improve your financial situation, rather than admit to yourself that its impossible. Your subconscious will just as readily respond to these positive commands as it will to the negative commands. Why programme yourself to fail?

We will attract to ourselves in actual physical reality, whatever we think most about. Here are some examples of negative self talk (to be avoided) Are you guilty of using any of these?

1. I can't afford it
2. I'm hopeless at remembering names
3. I've got a terrible memory
4. It's one of these days!
5. Knowing my luck . . .
6. I'm sick and tired of . . .
7. That really annoys me !
8. I'm too old for that
9. Bad things always happen in three's (superstition)
10. Why is it that every time I get ahead, something bad always happens?
11. I wasn't meant to succeed
12. Its alright for them! (indicating that it's not alright for you)
13. It goes in one hand and out the other (money)
14. Typical Monday morning!
15. Thank goodness its Friday! (indicating that all other weekdays are hellish)
16. Money doesn't grow on trees (indicating that there is a shortage)
17. Its just the way I am (indicating that you don't have the ability to change)
18. They're superior

These are just a few examples of probably hundreds of different sayings which are extremely destructive and cause us to fail. It's bad enough to fail but it's even worse when its self inflicted and based on falsehood. Changing your words can often be the 'little difference' that makes the big difference. Even if you've identified some areas where you are talking negatively to yourself, why not decide right now to change your words and start programming yourself for success instead?

The next time you catch yourself about to say something negative, STOP! And then THINK! Ask yourself "Is this what I want?" And if the answer is no, then don't say it. Instead figure out what you do want and say that. In response to the above examples, why not say :

1. I'll find a way to afford it
2. I'm great at remembering names (even if you're not, you will programme your subconscious to become so)
3. I've got a great memory
4. Things are going great!
5. Things always work out well for me
6. I love what I do
7. Instead of saying "That really annoys me" better to say nothing at all
8. Age is only a number. You're only as old as you think you are
9. Great and exciting things are happening every day
10. In this case, better to say nothing
11. I was born to win
12. Better to say nothing
13. I am getting richer and richer every day. Business is going great!
14. Every day is a gift from God. Life is exciting
15. I look forward to every day! Great things are happening everyday
16. I am wealthy. Thank you Father for my wealth.
17. I can be whatever I want to be. I have no limits
18. There are no superior or inferior. I'm as good as anyone else

By doing this, you will be instructing your subconscious to create what you want instead of what you don't want. So before you say anything, THINK!   And ask yourself, "Is this what I want?" And if the answer is no, don't say it.

CHAPTER 2

IS IT THE TRUTH?

The first response you usually get from people when suggesting saying what you want, as opposed to what you don't want, is "But I'm just telling the truth!" For example, if someone is in the habit of saying "I can't afford it", and someone suggests they start saying "I am wealthy, I am now making £100, 000 per year" (or whatever amount they desire to make), they may well look at you a bit strange. They usually protest because they feel they are lying to themselves. They say things like "But you don't understand, I really can't afford it!" But what they fail to realise is that our words have the power to change our reality. We can create a different reality by speaking different words. Think about it, would you use "I can't afford it" as an affirmation? Why not? Because you don't want that. So why say it now? It's all the same to your subconscious. Obviously if you are broke and you start saying I am now making £100,000 per year, things will not suddenly and magically change. But you will programme your subconscious to go in that direction and it will start to attract opportunities to bring it about. Your mind will be open, instead of shut. It may take quite some time to go from broke, to making £100, 000 per year, but don't look for instant results because they won't be instant. The important thing is that your subconscious has now changed direction and your mind is now open to it. If you say something often enough, it will become true. Your consciousness will become saturated with those thoughts and your subconscious has no choice but to respond. That's all it can respond to.

People who say "I can't afford it" don't realise they are contributing to their own misfortune by keeping themselves locked in a vicious cycle. It all starts with words. Words create your state of mind, which are picked up by your subconscious and are made real. Words are also the tools for breaking out of a limiting state of mind. Words can cause success or failure. As long as someone is saying "I can't afford it", it will be true for them, because their subconscious keeps getting the same commands and keeps creating the same results. What do you want to be true? That's what you need to ask yourself, and then say that.

NEGATIVE CYCLE (to be avoided)

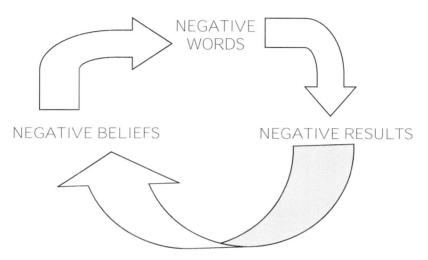

NEGATIVE WORDS

NEGATIVE BELIEFS

NEGATIVE RESULTS

The only way to change the cycle is by changing the words you speak. If a person has developed a lifelong habit of saying "I can't afford it", it will be so firmly embedded in their subconscious mind that it will now be accepted as the 'truth' by their subconscious. Their subconscious (their obedient servant) will also have been responding all those years by helping them to stay broke. Therefore, because they now have outward 'evidence' of being broke, it will be true for them and they will believe it. They now have 'proof' that they are broke, which serves to back up their words. Thus, the vicious cycle goes on.

Through sheer ignorance of how the mind works, they don't realise that they have contributed (and are contributing) to their own misfortune. Remember that the subconscious is a goal seeking mechanism which will go in any direction, but we decide the direction. I'm firmly convinced that if people knew the power of their words and their subconscious mind, they would be far more careful in how they programmed it. Maybe you are in the habit of saying" I can't afford it". If so, why not decide how much you want to make and start saying that instead? Obviously words are only part of the equation, you also need to take advantage of opportunity, and take some kind of action. Wealth won't automatically find you if you change your words but decide to sit at home watching TV. You need to do something.

POSITIVE CYCLE

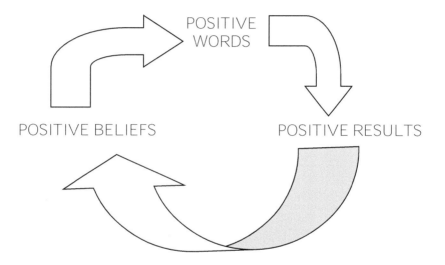

POSITIVE
WORDS

POSITIVE BELIEFS

POSITIVE RESULTS

Please don't misunderstand me, I'm not saying that you can simply speak positive words while doing foolish things with your money, and still expect your financial situation to improve. You still need to be doing wise things such as saving, tithing and possibly investing in order to reach you financial goal. But the words you speak, as well as your actions, help to create a 'wealth mentality' which create the results. There are many examples of people who went from poverty to great wealth, as a result of changing their words and their habits. So if a person who held the belief "I can't afford it" could become wealthy, then the original belief must have been false. Yet because they believe it, then it's true for them. Yes, it's possible to believe something which is false and self defeating, but this makes no difference to your subconscious mind, it responds to what you believe. If you believe it, then it's true for you. It might be worth examining your beliefs (in all areas) to see if you have any destructive or limiting beliefs. If you discover any, ask yourself why you believe the way you do? Where and when did it first originate? Is there any evidence to back it up? Could it be that you are mistaken and are unnecessarily contributing to your own misery? Challenge it, don't just accept it.

Some people believe that some people were born to succeed and others were born to fail. They believe that where you are, is where you stay and that's your slot in life. They may look at someone with envy, who has great wealth and think "It's alright for them, they were obviously born to be wealthy" This, again is an untruth but if they believe it, then it will be true for them. Some people say things like "I'll never be rich" or they may hold the secret belief that success is only meant for the other guy. In other words they accept that they were only meant to be mediocre or average at best. If they accept that, then it will be true for them, and it will be reflected in the outward results in their lives.

Most people who believe that we are pigeon-holed into certain slots in life, don't usually believe we have the ability to change ourselves, let alone change our circumstances. They think that life is about chance, instead of choice. They don't realise that it is chosen. It is impossible for a person to change inwardly, and not have their outward circumstances change also. Therefore, you can change your outer world by first changing your inner world. A persons outward circumstances in their life, is always a direct reflection of their inner world (which is their thinking) As one changes, so does the other. This can be good news or bad news, depending on your thinking. But if you're not happy with your outward circumstances, why not change your thinking? After all, it is your thinking that has created your circumstances up until now.

The greatest ability we, as human beings have, is the ability to change. If we couldn't change, we would be broke the rest of our lives, stuck with a poor self image and have no hope of developing self confidence. But fortunately, that is not the case. There are no limits to what you can achieve or become. It depends on what you tell yourself and whether you believe it or not. If you don't believe it, then your limiting beliefs will become like iron chains, restricting you, and binding you to the negativity of the past. There is nothing in your life, either inwardly or outwardly which cannot be changed, if you so desire. But please don't make the mistake of trying to change your outer world without first changing your inner world. It doesn't work that way. Your thinking must always change first, long before you see any outward evidence. The Bible says "The way of a fool seems right to him, but a wise man listens to advice" (Prov 12: 15)

We must always remember that what we tell ourselves is a choice and it is our responsibility to firstly identify it, and then change it if necessary. Many people, through ignorance of how the mind works, never even identify it, let alone do something about it. As a result, they limit themselves and spend their whole lives programming themselves for mediocrity or failure.

SO, WHAT IS THE TRUTH?

By now you might be wondering what exactly is the truth? and how does all this work? Well it really doesn't matter if something is true or not. If you believe it, then its true for you. Therefore, each one of us will have a different 'reality' because we all have a different set of beliefs. So, the important question is not so much "Is it true?" but "What do I believe?" because that will become your reality (even if it's not just now). I'll never forget the time when I had almost finished eating some tinned food. I noticed there was a slightly different taste, which could have been due to the fact that it was a different brand from normal. So I looked at the date on the bottom of the can and to my horror, it appeared to be several months out of date. Immediately I began to feel sick and realised that it was too late because I'd already eaten most of it.

But I thought I would check the date again, this time, a little closer. I then realised I had read the date wrong. What I thought was AUG 2006, was actually AUG 2008 I was alright! The food was alright too, since this was only November 2006! Immediately upon this change of belief, I was instantly healed. I didn't feel sick anymore. I was healed by belief, and the power of my mind. Yet, supposing I hadn't discovered the real date and was still convinced that the food was out of date? I would have continued to feel sick because of what I believed, even although it was a lie. In both cases, I felt sick and well, as a result of eating the same food. The food didn't change, only my beliefs. This proves a powerful point ; How I felt (my physical condition) had nothing to do with fact but everything to do with my beliefs. Belief can literally make us sick or well, regardless of 'facts'. Maybe that's why some people overcome so called 'terminal illnesses' and some don't. If a person believes (has faith) they can overcome it, then it is possible, regardless of 'facts'. But if they don't believe it, then they probably won't. Remember the words of Jesus; "Everything is possible for him who believes" (Mark 9: 23)

THOUGHT CAN MAKE YOU ILL OR WELL

We can see this same principle at work, regarding the 'placebo effect'. This is when people who are ill, are given sugar pills instead of real drugs, but they believe they are real drugs. Often these people get better after taking them, because they believe they are real drugs. But its obviously not the pills that heal them, because they are only sugar pills. They are healed because of belief. They believe the 'drugs' will make them better, and as a result, they get better. Remember that your subconscious creates according to belief, and is also responsible for healing you. What do you believe regarding your health? Do you believe that the older you get, the more your health deteriorates? If you've answered yes, your subconscious is already working on it right now to make it a reality. And if you talk about it, it only makes it more definite to your subconscious mind. When you talk about something, you give it life and you give it power. The

Bible says "The tongue has the power of life and death" (Prov 18 : 21) Never underestimate the power of words. What you say is what you get.

You might argue, "But it's true! The older you get, the more your health does deteriorate". Well if that's what you believe, then that will be true for you. Have you ever thought that its not because your health deteriorates that you believe it, but because you believe it that your health deteriorates? Think about it! Ask yourself why you believe the way you do? Are you looking at other people who have already reached a certain age and using them as an example? Are you expecting to follow in their footsteps? Remember, successful people look for successful examples. "Moses was a hundred and twenty years old when he died, yet his eyes were not weak nor his strength gone" (Deut 34 : 7) You also need to ask yourself "Is that what I want? Do I want my health to deteriorate as I get older?" If the answer is no, then don't say it. Even if it was a fact, your subconscious doesn't care about facts, remember? It only acts upon what you accept and believe. If you can get your head around this concept, you can programme your subconscious to work in your favour, in any area of your life, regardless of 'facts'. That means financially, your relationships, mentally and physically.

I remember when one of my relatives was ill and he said he had a touch of the flu and felt it coming on a few days ago. I realised right then and there that he had programmed his subconscious to get ill, firstly by accepting it and secondly by speaking words of illness. It was then 'made real' by his subconscious, and he did become ill. But you might be thinking "Maybe he really did feel ill and was only telling the truth?" Okay I take your point, but even if he did feel it coming on, he still had the free will to either accept it or reject it. To speak about it, or not to speak about it. To give it power or not to give it power.

Remember that what you accept does not have to be in alignment with the truth, in order for the subconscious to act on it. The subconscious controls the body, not the other way about. If you do feel something coming on, it is far better to say nothing than to programme yourself to get ill. You might think it sounds crazy speaking of yourself as healthy when your physical body says otherwise, but do you want to be in good health or not? That's what you need to ask yourself. If you are already up against it physically, why be up against it mentally as well?

Some people, afraid of getting the flu, go for the flu vaccine, in the hope that it will prevent them from catching it. Does it work? I don't know. I've never had it. I suppose a lot depends on whether you believe it works. If you believe that it will prevent you from getting the flu, it probably will. If you doubt it works, then you are more likely to catch the flu. Belief is everything. Belief can virtually perform the 'impossible', if one so believes. A person can also become ill because of suggestion. For example, if a person who was in perfect health went into work one morning and co-worker after co-worker kept commenting on how pale they looked, how do you think they would feel? At first they might not take it seriously and refuse to accept it, but if enough people kept on saying it, eventually they might start to believe it. They might start to think, "I must look bad, everybody keeps saying it. Perhaps I am ill?" And that's the danger point ; when you accept it! Because after that, your beliefs start to change. The subconscious then picks up the fact that you have accepted it, looks upon illness as a goal and then proceeds to bring it about. Was it the truth that they were ill? Absolutely not! But it became the truth, because of what they chose to believe. The fact was, they were healthy but the subconscious was given a goal of illness instead, so it had no choice but to go in that direction, regardless of facts.

Now that's the negative side, there's also a positive side. There has to be, because you can't have a minus without a plus, or a plus without a minus. If suggestions can make you ill, they can also make you well. Imagine a person wasn't feeling very well, and they also looked quite pale. Suddenly, person after person kept telling them how fit and healthy they looked. People would make comments such as "Have you been on holiday? You're looking tanned" Or they might say "You look a picture of health! What's the secret?" If a person received enough of these comments, eventually they would start to believe it. And once accepted, their subconscious would act upon it, and would seek to bring it about. In other words, there's a far higher chance of them making a quick recovery, if they have accepted positive thoughts, than negative thoughts.

So what do you do if you are ill? First of all, don't wait on other people to tell you how good you look because it probably won't happen. But you can, by using affirmations tell yourself how well you are, and how healthy you look. If you do this often enough, your subconscious mind will look upon health as a goal, and you have more chance of being healed. Words are often the best 'medicine' yet most people use them to create illness instead of health. In the third chapter I have included some examples which you can use to create health instead of illness, or you may want to use some of your own.

WHAT IS REAL?

Is there such a thing as objective reality? I don't know, because everyone has a different reality depending on their beliefs and perception. Therefore two different people could experience the exact same situation and have a completely different reality. For example, two different people could be in a room full of total strangers, and one person might perceive them as being friendly and helpful while the other person perceives them as being hostile and threatening. In both cases it is true for them because that is what they believe. But if there was such a thing as ob-jective reality, then it would be impossible for two different people to have a different reality because what is real for one, would be real for the other. But that is not the case. Therefore I believe in 'subjective reality'. I believe that our reality and our 'world' is subject to our beliefs and perception. If our beliefs change, our world changes accordingly. Shakespeare said, "There is nothing inherently good or bad, but thinking makes it so."

I remember hearing a veteran from the First World War talking about how he had lost sight of what was real. He had been fighting in the trenches for so long, that when he eventually came home on leave, he said there was something very 'unreal' about leave. He had got himself into a state of mind where the trenches was the 'real world' and being back home in London with his family was 'unreal'. When I heard that, I realised something ; in order to stay sane, we have to tell ourselves 'something', otherwise we might not know what the 'real world' is. Your world will always be in accordance with your most dominant thoughts. Your most dominant thoughts have the biggest emotional impact. This, then becomes your 'world'.

In the same way, if we've had negative habits and a negative mindset for most of our lives, then we will only have ever experienced a 'negative world'. But if we start to develop positive habits and a positive mindset, we will start to experience a positive world. But hold on a minute, surely the world hasn't changed? How can we experience two different 'worlds?' Surely the world is just the same now, as it was before? Yes, it is still the same objectively, but in your case it has changed (subjectively) And that's what matters. Everyone has a different 'world'. The point I am trying to make is this ; whatever your mind becomes saturated with, whether positive or negative, becomes your 'world'. It makes no difference what the objective world, outside is like, it has no bearing on your subjective world. That, then becomes true for you.

Psychiatrist Gerald Jampolsky M.D, explains in his book "Love Is Letting Go Of Fear" that our mind can be likened to a motion picture camera, projecting our internal state onto the world. He goes on to say that perception is a mirror, not a fact. We don't see things as 'they' are, we see them as we are. As we change, so does our perception. If we have fearful thoughts, then we will see everything and everyone in it, as making us fearful. But if we have positive, happy thoughts, then we will see everything and everyone in it as positive and happy.

But our emotions also play a major role in how we perceive the world. Negative emotions such as fear, lust, anxiety, anger and hatred distort our perception and cause us to perceive other people negatively, while positive emotions such as love, romance, faith, hope and enthusiasm cause us to perceive other people positively. What we see in ourselves, we will see in other people. How we view ourselves is how we will view the world. This should be viewed as good news, because even if you don't like the way you see yourself (at the moment), it means we have the freedom to change our world by changing ourselves.

For example, supposing a person holds the belief that they are terrible at public speaking, then at that precise moment, that is true for them. But when that same person, a few years later, becomes a confident public speaker, their belief system will have changed to "I am a confident public speaker". And because they believe it, that will now be true for them. In other words, because their beliefs have changed, so has their reality. The subconscious has no 'fixed reality', it responds to what is believed at the present moment even if it totally contradicts previous beliefs. So if a person's 'reality' can change according to their beliefs, it means that many of us are walking around at this very moment, believing self destructive things unnecessarily. How many of us, at this precise moment believe lies about ourselves?

WE CREATE OUR CIRCUMSTANCES

For example, a person may believe that they are inferior to other people. Or they may believe that they are superior and other people are inferior. Both beliefs are false because there is no such thing as an inferior or superior person. Admittedly, some people may be more talented at certain things, but they are not a superior person. Instead, they are an ordinary person with extraordinary gifts. But remember that you also have gifts which other people don't have, so the truth is, we are all just different and unique. God didn't create some people to succeed and some people to fail; He created every one of us with unique gifts and talents, with the potential to become great. He also put the seeds of greatness within every one of us. But it's up to us to develop those 'seeds' and develop our potential. But unfortunately, not everyone does that. How can we possibly appreciate our self worth by degrading it and talking badly about it? We can't. How can we possibly develop more of our potential by talking negatively to ourselves? We can't, and we won't. How can we possibly discover the greatness God has put inside of us by saying things like "I've not got what it takes" or "It's alright for them, they've got more confidence than me". How can we improve if we are saying things like "I've got a terrible memory". We can't. Not only does it damage our own self image, but it also dishonours God. We are all Gods creations, He created us in His own image and God does not make inferior products. Some of us may suffer from inferior thinking, but that should not demean the product. Remember that our thinking is something we can change if we so desire.

"So God created man in his own image,
in the image of God he created him;
male and female he created them"
(Gen 1: 27)

If we want to improve our lives and change our reality, we must look inwardly, not outwardly. Many people make the big mistake of trying to improve their lives by focusing only on external things, but if this is the only focus, it only leads to frustration and unhappiness. The focus must be on changing ourselves and changing our beliefs. If and when we do that, external things will take care of themselves and be seen as simply by-products of success.

Negative or inferior thinking is something which we learn as we go through life. Very often, negative self talk is the result of us having failed at something. Sometimes it can be the result of criticism from other people. If accepted, we then come to the conclusion that we are not good at that particular thing. Or even worse, we might tell ourselves that we are inadequate or not capable of improving. The danger is 'mentally accepting' it as a fact because then it becomes true for you. If you want to improve your self image, you need to learn to refuse to accept anything which is degrading or destructive. You need to become mentally tough and develop the ability to let criticism 'bounce off' you. You need to realise that because you may have failed, you are not a 'failure'. You must understand the difference. The difference is huge. Never accept anything which detracts from your self image. Never let someone else's negative opinion of you become your reality.

Have you ever noticed that the image we have of ourselves, is often the image we believe other people have of us? This is often linked to our behaviour in their presence. If we have previously behaved in a respectful manner in their presence, then when we find ourselves in their presence at a later date, our inner voice will be "I am a respectful person" because that is what I believe, they believe about us. It's all to do with beliefs, (and often 'mind games').

I once heard a saying which I thought summed it up;

"I'm not what I think I am,
I'm not what you think I am,
but I am what I think, you think I am"
(Anonymous)

We talk to ourselves all the time, and most of the time we are not even aware of it. But usually we are our own worst critic. For example, a person may aspire to become an artist and enrol in a college course. At the end of the course they have an exam, and although, generally their work was good throughout the year, they fail the actual exam. As a result they come to the conclusion that they were 'not meant' to be an artist, and tell themselves, and everybody else that they are hopeless at art. As a result of failing the test, they allow their inner voice to take a negative direction and label themselves as 'hopeless' at that particular thing, even although their work was generally good. Once you accept such a label, you make it final as far as your subconscious mind is concerned and you close off all possibilities for improvement and you limit your potential. This doesn't mean there is any truth in it, but as long as you accept it and believe it, then it's true for you. In other words, you believe a lie about yourself.

Instead of telling yourself you're not good at a particular thing, why not tell yourself "I just haven't taken the time to learn it yet" There's a big difference. One closes off opportunity for improvement, the other keeps the door open. One involves possibility thinking, the other involves 'impossibility thinking'. Either way it will be true for you.

A person under hypnosis may be in a room where the temperature is 20 Celsius, but if he is convinced that the temperature is minus 20 Celsius, his body will show every physical symptom that would normally occur, if it were actually minus 20 Celsius. Shivering may occur and they will actually 'feel cold' because of what they believe, even though the actual room is warm. These bodily reactions are a subconscious response to what they believe. Remember, the subconscious doesn't care about facts, it responds to belief, even if the belief is the complete opposite of the 'truth'.

We can turn this to our advantage by saying to ourselves "Does that mean if I don't feel very well (fact), that if I can convince my subconscious otherwise, that it will respond to what I tell it, even if it contradicts the fact that I don't feel very well?" Yes, that's exactly what I'm saying and that is exactly how the subconscious works. But most people don't do that. They don't use it to their advantage; instead they use it to their disadvantage by telling everyone how bad they feel. Either way, it becomes their reality. So how do I convince my subconscious that I'm feeling good when I'm not? We do it by words. If you say something often enough, eventually it will be accepted by your subconscious mind. If you don't feel too good, don't say that or you will create it. Why not say "I feel great" instead? What have you got to lose? You will never go wrong by speaking words of health. The question you always need to ask yourself is "Is this what I want?" If the answer is no, then don't say it. Your words create your reality, even if it is the complete opposite to your present 'reality'. But I must also point out that our emotional state is also a major factor in keeping good health. If you can avoid all negative emotions and practice having only positive emotions, (this can only be done by having positive actions and habits) then this will go a long way towards keeping in good health. More about this later.

We spoke earlier about how two different people can have a

different reality in the same room full of strangers, based on their perception and beliefs. The interesting thing is that both people will be able to give you 'evidence' or 'proof', to back up their beliefs. If one person perceives the people there to be friendly and helpful, but the other perceives them to be hostile and threatening, they will both be able to give you real life accounts to 'prove' their beliefs right. They don't realise that life is a mirror and gives us back exactly what we project into it. Therefore, what they saw in other people will be a reflection of how they projected themselves.

One could probably give you a detailed description of how people went out of their way to make them feel welcome and bent over backwards to help them, while the other could give you a vivid description of how people ignored them and how hostile people were towards them. These 'incidents' only serve to reinforce their original beliefs, which is all very well if your state of mind is positive, but not so good if its negative. We cannot help but see in other people what we see in ourselves. Our perception is based on our beliefs, but because everyone's beliefs are different, everyone has a different 'reality'. Remember, the subconscious has no objective reality, but you can change your reality by changing what you allow into your mind, which in turn, changes your emotional state. But we also need to take into account the individual's attitude towards the other people, because people usually respond in kind. But here's the key; our state of mind determines what we project. If our state of mind is negative, we cannot help but project negativity. Thus, we will experience a 'negative world'. Often people who project negativity, don't realise they are doing it and they can't understand why people are responding negatively to them. But if your state of mind is positive, then you will project this also, and people will respond positively to you. (A different reality in the same situation)

PERCEPTION

Obviously what we are talking about here is perception. People perceive differently from each other, based on their own psyche and mindset. Your emotions are very powerful and can either enhance or distort your perception, depending on whether your emotions are positive or negative. When your emotions are positive, your perception is in alignment with the truth and you can experience a beautiful world, but when your emotions are negative, your perception is distorted and ugly, but unfortunately just as real nevertheless. The solution? Control your emotional state!

When people perceive things differently, it's not that one person is right and the other is wrong. As far as their subconscious mind is concerned they are both 'right', only different. As we change, so does our perception. Just to illustrate how our perception changes according to what we believe, I remember when I had an appointment to show a business presentation to a couple who lived in what was called a 'rough neighbourhood'. I had heard a lot of bad stories about the place and people were saying to me, "If you go there, you won't get back out in one piece". Someone else said "Don't expect your car to have any wheels left when you come back out!" As a result, I was a bit apprehensive but I went anyway because I knew that the only way to become successful was to face your fears. As I drove through the neighbourhood, I viewed everyone with suspicion and potentially hostile. I even sensed a sort of tense atmosphere in the air. When I got to the couples house, they were very friendly and as we got chatting, I said "What's it like staying down here?" They said "Its fine, the people are really nice. We've stayed here for a couple of years and we like it". Right then and there, I had a paradigm shift (my beliefs changed) and I no longer had the same perception of it because of the change in my beliefs. As a result of a successful presentation, I ended up visiting their house a couple of times a week. Each time I drove through the neighbourhood my perception of the people walking the streets changed a little each time. After a while, I didn't view them with suspicion anymore and there no longer seemed to be a tense atmosphere in the air. Probably due to the fact that it wasn't real but imaginary, fabricated in the workshop of my mind. (fabricated according to belief) My car also emerged intact after each visit, wheels and all!

Now that is an example of perception according to our conscious thinking, but perception can go deeper than that when it involves our emotions. If you are suffering from negative emotions, the emotions you experience affects what you actually see with your eyes. For example, if you are suffering from anger, you will see other people with angry faces. If you are happy, you will see other people with happy, smiling faces. If you are suffering from the emotion of lust, as a result of sexual immorality, you will see sleaziness in other people. Whatever image you have of yourself, you will see in other people. The truth is, the world is a mirror of ourselves. If we are friendly towards other people, then there's a good chance they will be friendly towards us. But if we view people as suspicious and hostile, then that's exactly what will happen in reality.

A person who is overweight might not perceive themselves as overweight, instead they might perceive other people as being thin. Why? Because we always see things in comparison to ourselves. Whatever we look at, we see according to how we are. Yet, if that same person were to lose weight, they might not perceive other people as being thin anymore; instead they might perceive them as being 'just right'. Yet the other people haven't changed, it was them who changed.

SUPERSTITION

Superstition is about beliefs which are based on falsehood and is clearly condemned in the Bible. (see Deut 18 : 10-12) Yet many people put their faith in superstition instead of Almighty God. Some people put their faith in good luck charms and omens. Others put their faith in clairvoyants and mediums. Some people think the number thirteen is unlucky, and it is unlucky to walk under a ladder. But do these things come true? It depends on whether you believe it or not. Remember that your subconscious creates according to belief. Whatever you believe, you will attract. This will be true for you, even if it based on falsehood, because your subconscious will attract it. This is the principle of the self-fulfilling prophecy and is also Satan's way of deceiving us. You might think, "But how is it Satan's way of deceiving us?" The answer is because it takes us away from God. I've never met anyone who goes to church and also goes to clairvoyants. It has been my experience that it's always one or the other. Therefore, if Satan can get us to put our faith in superstition, he can take us away from God.

Some people are deceived by mediums and clairvoyants because of their accuracy, and I do admit that the vast majority of them are very accurate and do have powers. But people underestimate the power of the devil. Did you know that the Devil has the power to perform miracles? The Bible says "The coming of the lawless one will be in accordance with the work of Satan displayed in all kinds of counterfeit miracles, signs and wonders, and in every sort of evil that deceives those who are perishing. They perish because they refused to love the truth and so be saved." (2 Thes 2: 9-10)

Therefore if Satan wants to suck us in, he has to give clairvoyants and mediums the power to be accurate, because if everything they said was false, no-one would be deceived by them. For example, a clairvoyant may be 95 percent accurate, but the 5 percent will take you away from God. They may be able to tell you names of dead friends and relatives, along with other facts and figures, but in actual fact, it causes people to trust in them, rather than turn to God in prayer. That's exactly what the Devil wants!

People are amazed by their accuracy and will often make a habit of visiting clairvoyants frequently, and will blindly believe whatever they are told. After they have been told a certain amount of 'accurate details' the clairvoyant could tell them virtually anything, and they would believe it. Their reasoning is that because so much of the information has been accurate so far, then surely everything must be true.

Some people are in the habit of calling the dead, which is clearly condemned by God. For example, a person may try to communicate with their dead aunt. They go through their rituals and ask the spirit (their aunt) questions. They receive very accurate answers and so they believe they are communicating with their dead aunt. Because of the accuracy of the answers, they are absolutely convinced it is their dead aunt. They don't realise that they may be communicating instead, with the Devil, pretending to be their aunt. They think they know, but they don't really know. Remember, the Devil is a trickster and a liar, and is far too powerful for us. That's why we need to turn to God in prayer, because He is the only one who can deal with the him.

People who are superstitious also give direction to their subconscious mind by the words they speak. For example, if they've walked under a ladder, they might say "Oh no! I've just walked under a ladder. That's bad luck". And subconsciously, they are on the lookout for something bad to happen. They might even start to tell other people in the course of conversation, that they walked under a ladder and something bad will probably happen. Is it surprising then, if something bad does happen? Not really, because as they speak these words, it is picked up by their subconscious and looked upon as a 'goal'. They don't realise that the words we speak, have the power to create and attract whatever we speak about. If and when something 'bad' does happen, it only serves to reinforce their belief in superstition.

There are people who will refuse to buy a house if it has the number thirteen on the door. When it comes to Friday the thirteenth, they often say "Oh no! its Friday the thirteenth today" and they expect bad things to happen. Or, if a person who walks under a ladder does have some 'bad luck' later that day, they usually equate it to the act of walking under the ladder. But it was not the act of walking under the ladder which caused it; it was the 'belief about the act' which caused it. Although, many of them will not believe that. Therefore, if a person who wasn't superstitious walked under a ladder, it would have no effect on them because their beliefs are different. A truly positive thinker will happily sit down to dinner at a table for thirteen people.

You also need to realise that superstition is a form of fear, and fear is highly destructive. You cannot be truly successful if you allow fear to control you. Whatever you have fear of, can do you no harm unless you allow it. We should take heed of the fact that Jesus words are the truth, not necessarily the words of men.

Jesus said "I am the way, and the truth and the life, no-one comes to the Father except through me" (John 14 : 6) Jesus is the one and only way in which we can know the truth, and the only way by which we can be saved. Therefore, if there are any 'old wives tales' or anything which contradicts the Bible, then it is based on falsehood. Think about it, you cannot have two opposing 'truths'. If they contradict each other, one must be false. People who put their faith in mediums and clairvoyants are playing right into the hands of the Devil, because putting your faith in any other mediator except Jesus Christ, does not lead to God. "For there is one God and one mediator between God and men, the man Jesus Christ" (1 Tim 2: 5).

The Bible also tells us "According to your faith will it be done to you" (Mat 9: 29) Therefore, depending on your faith (or lack of it) we have the power to influence the results in our lives, to a large degree. If you have faith, you will see results, if you don't have faith, then don't expect to see results. When Jesus healed the blind men, notice how He first asked them if they believed He could do it (Mat 9: 27-29) When they answered yes, a healing took place. But belief also has a flip side to it. Belief in a thing makes it happen, while lack of belief (or lack of faith) does the opposite. In the book of Matthew we are told, "And He did not do many miracles there because of their lack of faith" (Mat 13: 58) So the important question to ask ourselves is, not so much "Is it the truth?" but "What do I believe?"

43

CHAPTER 3

EVERYTHING AFFECTS YOUR SUBCONSCIOUS

Some time ago, there was an experiment carried out at a cinema which involved the use of the subconscious mind, although the people in the cinema were completely unaware of what was happening. During the film, the words "popcorn" and "Coca cola" were flashed up on the screen as people watched the film. It was done at such a high speed that it was impossible to see with the naked eye, but the interesting thing was that the subconscious picked it up! The result was, at the interval, there was a vast increase in the sales of popcorn and Coca Cola. These people were unaware that their subconscious mind had been affected at an emotional level by the words on the screen. Their emotion of desire had been affected by what their subconscious had picked up. As a result, they had the desire to purchase popcorn or Coca Cola, (or both) without knowing why they got the urge. Awesome is the power of the subconscious! Yet many people still claim that TV doesn't affect them.

We need to be aware that we, as humans, are primarily motivated by our emotions. ALL input which reaches our brain, through the five senses, has an effect on our subconscious mind and our emotions. For example, seeing a tropical beach on TV or seeing a picture of your dream car, might appeal to your emotion of desire. It may go further than that, and cause you to take action and buy that car, or go to that place. All that can happen, simply as a result of seeing a picture or a 30 second advertisement, which influences your emotions. Seeing a gloomy weather forecast can cause you to feel disappointed or even depressed, especially if you were planning a day out. If you are buying a birthday card for your spouse and you see the ideal card in a shop, you will probably experience the emotions of love and romance. If you hear about an injustice, it can cause you to experience anger, simply as a result of what you have heard. If you are walking in the countryside, in the pitch dark and you hear a growling noise, it can cause you to experience the emotion of fear. These are just a few examples of probably hundreds of potential situations which affect our emotions on a daily basis. Yet for most of us, the thought of whether our emotions are an influential part of our behaviour probably never even crosses our minds. Not only do our emotions influence our behaviour, but our behaviour also influences our emotions. It works both ways. All our actions create an emotional response from our subconscious mind. For example, if you were to put on a grumpy face and go around the house slamming doors, you would start to feel angry because of your actions, even though you had nothing to be angry about. Remember that your sub-conscious doesn't know the difference between a real experience and one vividly imagined. But just for the sake of a positive example, go to the privacy of your room, stand up straight, smile and start waving, as if you are waving to a friend, and shout "Hello!" and see if this makes you feel happier. It does, doesn't it? Because your actions affect your emotions.

YOU DIDN'T GET YOUR FACE BY ACCIDENT

Your facial expression is a result of your lifelong attitudes, words and emotions. The long term effect of this is quite profound. Have you ever seen someone with a beautiful smiling face, who constantly moans and complains? I doubt it. Have you ever seen someone with a grumpy face who is the life and soul of the party? I doubt it either, because our emotions are always telling on us and the results show in our faces. Try saying "It's a miserable day outside" with a smile. Try saying "What a beautiful day!" with a frown. It's very difficult isn't it? Because they don't add up. Therefore, a person with a frown face has probably developed it by their attitudes and words, over a sustained period of time. Likewise, a person with a happy face has probably developed it by a positive attitude, using positive words, which create positive emotions.

Happy faces and sour expressions don't come by accident.

They are developed, by habitual words, attitudes and emotional responses. It is possible for a person with a happy face to gradually develop a sour face, if they allowed their attitude to become negative. Conversely, it is possible for a person with a sour face to develop a beautiful smiling face, if they changed their attitude and their words, although the change would be very gradual.

Do you realise that you are the sum total of your thoughts? You are the sum total of all your emotions, your words, your experiences and your actions? You are the sum total of all your beliefs? All of these things comprise who you are, as a person. Change these things and you change the person. Obviously we cannot change the past, but we can change what we do from this moment onwards. That is within your control and always will be. Whatever thoughts you are thinking just now, is having an effect on your subconscious mind. Have you ever noticed that if a negative thought or idea crosses your mind, it causes you to feel depressed? That's because the emotion of depression is a subconscious response to your conscious thinking. But if you suddenly think a good positive thought, the emotion of happiness is the response.

If, for the sake of an example, you are in a negative state of mind, it's a good idea to examine what thoughts you have been thinking. Or maybe even more importantly, what actions have you been taking, which has caused these emotions? For example, if a man has been unfaithful to his wife, deep down, he won't be happy because he will be suffering from the emotion of lust. Lust cannot co-exist with happiness because it is a negative emotion. There's also a good chance he will be suffering from guilt, and possibly worry (worrying about being caught). This would make happiness impossible. In fact, I would go as far as to say it would make your life hell. Happiness can only come, as a result of positive emotions.

But if this same man was to stop that behaviour, ask God's forgiveness, then these negative emotions would disappear, and he would regain the emotion of happiness. Happiness is simply the absence of negative emotions. Happiness is our natural state. We destroy our own happiness, by our negative behaviour. If you look at the following lists of emotions, none of the negative emotions are compatible with happiness. Each and every one of them kill happiness. All emotions happen for a reason. So you need to retrace your steps (mentally) to find out the root cause. If it is behaviour which caused negative emotions, then you need to eliminate that behaviour. When you eliminate the be-**haviour, you will eliminate the emotions. That's why our habits** are so vitally important, and can make or break us. For example, reading a newspaper will normally cause you to think negative thoughts, which in turn, affects your emotions. Therefore if you eliminate reading newspapers, you will feel happier. Our habits are so numerous that it makes sense to analyse every area. Any habit which is fuelled by, or causes negative emotions is a failure habit that needs to be broken. Napoleon Hill covers the emotions in his book, Think and Grow Rich. I have also listed the most powerful emotions here, and have added a few more.

POSITIVE	NEGATIVE (to be avoided)
Love	Fear
Desire	Worry
Sex	Anxiety
Faith	Guilt
Hope	Lust
Romance	Depression
Enthusiasm	Greed
Courage	Hatred
	Anger
	Superstition
	Jealousy
	Self pity
	Revenge
	Doubt

The reason I have not listed happiness in the positive emotions is because happiness (although positive) cannot be pursued. It can only come as a result of doing positive things. Therefore it is a by-product. But if you practice behaviour which is fuelled by positive emotions, you will experience happiness. For example, you can do things for people out of love and this will result in happiness, but you cannot do something out of happiness, because happiness is always the result of something. You will notice that the emotion of sex is on the positive side and the emotion of lust is on the other. This is because the two are often confused with each other, so please don't think I am advocating the misuse of sex. God created sex to be good, but to be enjoyed only within marriage. But often confused with the positive emotion of sex, are negative sexual habits which are fuelled by lust, such as pornography, fornication, adultery and sexual unfaithfulness. Many people addicted to such behaviour, are going through life unhappy, without really knowing why they are unhappy. They don't realise that their own negative behaviour is destroying their happiness. They may be eluded into thinking they will be happier, but it is a trap. That is precisely how the devil works, he tricks us, lies to us and deceives us.

RESPONDING POSITIVELY TO NEGATIVE EMOTIONS

I mentioned that all emotions happen for a reason, which is true, but sometimes we find ourselves in situations which cause us to experience negative emotions such as fear. The fact that we experience fear is not our fault. For example, if you are faced with an opportunity to speak in public, it could cause you to experience fear. The fear is not your fault, but your response to the fear is your fault. You need to understand the difference between what you can and can't control. The situation you are in is beyond your control. You can't control what happens to you, but your response is within your control. This is 'crunch time'. This is what makes or breaks you. You only have two options; respond with courage or allow the fear to control you. At a time when you find yourself in the midst of fear, how you respond is everything. Taking action (responding with courage) is the only way to destroy fear.

Although what happens to us is important, our response is

even more important, because this is what will affect your self image and your inner voice. Be not so concerned about what happened to you, but be more concerned about how you responded to what happened to you. Instead of getting depressed because something bad happened to you, concentrate on how you responded to it. Did you respond positively or negatively? If you responded positively, don't worry about it. That's all you can do! Everything else is beyond your control. Learn to focus less on what happens, and more on how you respond. As long as you respond positively, your self image still improves. In fact I will go a stage further and say that we actually need adversity for our self image to improve, because it is only in these times of trials that we are strengthened. How could a soldier ever become a good soldier without experiencing the reality of war? For it is only in the tough times that they are strengthened. I remember hearing about a group of US marines who had landed on one of the Pacific islands during World War Two. These new marines were raw recruits with no battle experience. Suddenly they were faced with the horror of war; fanatical resistance from Japanese who preferred death to surrender. Banzai charges from Japanese troops who charged with swords against machine guns and flamethrowers. Within a few months, these 'new recruits' were battle hardened troops. They were strengthened because they responded with courage to extreme adverse circumstances.

I am also reminded of the story of a woman I shall call Jane. Jane did not get on well with her partner and he was often verbally abusive to her. Often when he phoned her, he would curse and swear and criticise her. These situations were causing Jane to feel depressed. But the reason she was getting so depressed was that instead of responding positively, she was responding negatively. She was allowing negative emotions to control her response. Each time he swore at her, she would start swearing back (responding with anger to adversity) which only made her worse. In a situation like that, there are two main positive options; firstly keep calm and be polite, so that you don't drop your level to their level. Secondly, tell them that you are not going to tolerate any more of that kind of abuse and that if it doesn't stop; it's the end of the relationship. It might mean the end of the relationship but at least your emotions will still be positive and your self image can only improve, as a result of such a positive stance.

EMOTIONALLY DRIVEN BEHAVIOUR

Emotions can mean the difference between success and failure, happiness or misery, health or illness, poverty or wealth. We are all creatures of habit and our habits usually fall into one of two main categories; either constructive or destructive (positive or negative) Our emotions are therefore an excellent guide in determining whether our habits are positive or negative. For example, if a habit causes us to feel guilty, it doesn't take much brains to figure out that it is a failure habit. Just because everyone else behaves in a certain way, doesn't necessarily make it right. Very often it has been a single negative habit which has caused the downfall of a person. For example, a person may have achieved a certain level of success and then turned to alcohol or drugs, only to lose everything. Or it could be that they've never had any success at all, and alcohol could be standing in their way. Either way it's destructive. It could be drugs, it could be pornography or sexual unfaithfulness and it could be anything. But it only takes one failure habit to bring a person down.

If you are in doubt as to whether a habit is positive or negative, don't take counsel from your friends or from the TV, instead see what the Bible has to say. Jesus warns us not to be conformed to 'the world'. Instead, "Enter through the narrow gate. For wide is the gate and broad is the road that leads to destruction, and many enter through it. But small is the gate and narrow the road that leads to life and only a few find it. (Mat 7: 13-14)

Most of our actions are driven by our emotions. When you think about it, what makes you do what you do? The fact that you are reading this book just now is because you DESIRE to learn something. But it's not just the big choices we make that are driven by our emotions, but everything, including small things. For example, you might rush to get to work because you FEAR being late, or you might go the extra mile at work because you HOPE you are going to get a promotion.

Emotionally driven behaviour means that the emotion comes first, before the act. For example a person might decide to buy a gift for their spouse because of LOVE. The loving thought came before the act of buying the gift. As a negative example (which I do not recommend), a person who is motivated by REVENGE, has the evil thought before they commit the act. Thus, the evil deed is based on a negative emotion.

When we have committed the act, the emotion which fuelled the act to begin with, will also dominate our thinking after the act. That's because our actions speak so loudly to our subconscious mind. Actions are so powerful that there's no way that our subconscious mind cannot be affected by it. The key? Make sure everything you do is based on, or is driven by positive emotions. If you get the seed of thought in your mind to do something which is based on negative emotions, resist it at all costs. This is often the devil trying to tempt us. Don't fall for it. It will only result in further negative emotions, such as guilt, fear or worry. This will adversely affect your self image, your beliefs about yourself, and will cause you even more problems. As a result, you will not be happy either. It might be worth going back a few pages and looking at the list of emotions and checking what your behaviour is based on. Refer to it often and use it as a guide.

If you avoid negative emotions, as far as possible and practice behaviour which is based only on positive emotions, you won't go far wrong. Equally important is making sure that your words are also based on positive emotions. For example, rather than speaking words of doubt, fear, or anger, we should speak words of faith, hope and enthusiasm. This will then create corresponding emotions. For example, rather than say "Knowing my luck, I'll probably fail" (doubt), it is far better to say "Things are going great! I succeed in everything I do" (faith). To the average person, the difference between those two sentences might not seem like a big deal, but it actually 'is' a big deal. In fact it is a huge deal, because most people underestimate the power of words. Notice how the first sentence is based on doubt and the second sentence is based on faith. The key to impressing something on your subconscious is repetition. The more times the words are spoken, the more of a compounding effect it will have on your subconscious mind and your emotional state. Repetition (in anything) has an accumulative effect on your subconscious. This is what I refer to as the 'little difference' which makes the big difference. If you learn to control your behaviour, you will learn to control your emotions.

We all speak thousands of words each and every day. Therefore it is of major importance that our words are positive, because of the accumulative effect. We are either going to be miles off (in a negative direction) or propelling ourselves in a positive direction towards our dreams. The type of language we use is also habit forming and therefore 'emotion forming'. Therefore someone in the habit of using negative words (swear words included), will be in a constant negative emotional state, thus making true happiness impossible. But someone who is in the habit of using only positive words will be in a constant state of 'high', the vast majority of the time. This emotional state, and way of thinking, becomes habitual, and influences the results in our lives. And on the cycle goes, whether it is positive or negative.

The emotions you create, as a result of your behaviour also have an effect on your physical health. That's why it's so important to develop and maintain a positive emotional state. Negative emotions weaken your immune system and drain your energy, while positive emotions strengthen your immune system and increase your energy. People who constantly speak words of pessimism, criticism, hatred, jealousy and anger etc. are actually contributing to their own misery, in more ways than one. But people who speak positively by encouraging other people, building them up, complimenting them, speaking words of faith, love, hope and enthusiasm, are actually contributing to their own mental and physical well being. When you compliment another person, it's almost as if you are complimenting yourself because of the positive emotions you create. Try it and see! Why not make a habit of complimenting at least one person every day? When you are talking with people, why not go out of your way to actually look for things to compliment. And if you see someone with a new hairstyle, or a new top, or nice sun-tan, tell them! They'll be delighted to hear it and you'll feel good too.

Some people create an 'illness mentality' by speaking words of illness, as soon as they feel the slightest touch of something coming on. Instead of depriving the 'ailment' of power by refusing to recognise it, they give it major recognition, firstly by mentally accepting it, and secondly by speaking about it.

Remember that when something is accepted by the conscious, it is 'made real' by the subconscious because that's the 'job' of the subconscious. Never mentally accept something you don't want, as this will become your reality. Instead, speak only words of health, as this will create a 'health mentality'. If you speak words of health whenever you feel an ailment coming on, you will stand a much higher chance of fighting it off because your subconscious will be working in your favour, instead of against you. No matter how bad it is, refuse to accept it. Why? Because the moment you accept it, you are admitting defeat and your subconscious will start to work against you. Operate in the mindset of faith and hope, that you are going to stay in good health and that the ailment will disappear as quickly as it came. This might sound like a paradox, but most people who get ill, have actually accepted that they are ill. Before you get annoyed at me, remember that we all have total control over our thoughts, 24 hours a day. Although a person may be ill physically, they do not have to accept it mentally, because they have free will. If they wanted to, they could choose to allow only thoughts of perfect health into their minds and refuse to entertain thoughts of illness. They could choose to speak words of health, while they were ill physically, and defy the illness instead of surrendering to it. This is one of the keys to staying in good health ; refuse to surrender to illness. There is also a psychological reason for this ; it is hard for your subconscious to act upon something which you don't recognise or accept.

I remember hearing about a woman who had been diagnosed with a 'terminal illness' and although she had a disease physically, she point blank refused to accept it mentally. Why? Because she refused to provide a goal of illness for her subconscious mind. She knew she couldn't expect health by accepting illness. She even started telling people she was cured before she was cured. She started thanking God for healing her, before she was healed. Obviously she had no guarantees that she would be healed, but she had faith. She only allowed her mind to focus on good health. And in the end she did get healed. Yet most people will scoff at this because they do not understand how the mind works. But why surrender? Why give in? Why provide a negative goal for your subconscious? Whatever the most dominant images you hold in your mind, your subconscious looks upon as a goal to achieve. If you accept that you are ill, then illness becomes the 'goal. But it is also possible to be ill physically and still have a positive goal mentally, by refusing to accept illness. This is what is often referred to as the 'Never Say Die' attitude which Winston Churchill was so famous for. Never ever get to a point where you allow your subconscious to work against you.

Your 'job' if you'll pardon the expression, is to convince your subconscious that only good health exists, and you certainly won't do that by thinking and speaking about illness. You need to starve your subconscious of all kinds of negative words and thoughts of illness, so that you will deprive it of a negative goal. Instead, you need to speak only positive words of health. Emotionally charged words such as ; strength, excellent health, physically fit, looking good, feeling good, on top of the world, energetic, all affect your subconscious in a positive way.

If you're not feeling too good, why not say:
"I am strong and energetic"
"I feel great!"
"I'm getting stronger and stronger every day"
"Every day I'm getting better and better"
"I am physically fit and in peak performance"
"I am in excellent health"
"People keep commenting on how good I look"

That's a whole lot better than telling everyone you don't feel too good. Wouldn't you agree? If you say the words "I don't feel too good", it actually causes you to feel depressed. Why do that to yourself? Don't the above examples cause you to feel better about yourself? Of course they do! You can actually speak something into existence which didn't exist before, by changing your words. And when you change your words, you will start to change your emotional state. You can speak words of health, happiness and prosperity, or you can speak yourself into an early grave. It's your choice. Think before you speak, and ask yourself "Do I want my subconscious to make this a reality? If the answer is "No" then don't say it. If the answer is "Yes" by all means, say it. Always use your words to your advantage!

IF YOU WANT TO STAY YOUNG, ACT YOUNG

Our behaviour (actions), as well as our words also have a major impact on our subconscious mind. Everything we say and do affects our emotional state. Our emotions, then affect our physical bodies. That's why you can often tell someone's emotional state by looking at their face. But it's not just our faces which are affected by our emotions. The whole of our bodies get affected, whether we are aware of it or not. Our subconscious is responsible for the renewal of every cell in our bodies, and therefore the ageing process. But we provide the initial direction for our subconscious by what we tell it and also by the indirect messages it receives, as a result of our behaviour.

Our subconscious knows the motive behind every action. For example, if you decide to stop doing something because you think you are 'too old', then being 'too old' is what your subconscious will accept and act upon. Many people alter their behaviour as they get older, thus reinforcing the message to their subconscious that they are getting old. On the other hand, I know people who have reached a certain age in life (which some people might consider to be 'old') and still look young because they have not allowed 'age' to change their behaviour or their habits. In other words, they still continue to act young. They continue to do the things which they have always done, which reinforces the message to their subconscious that they are still young and nothing has changed. It is therefore not surprising that they continue to look young.

I remember hearing a woman saying that she thought she was too old to sunbathe. It saddened me to hear her saying that, because firstly she was a good looking woman with as nice a body as someone half her age. And secondly I knew the damage she was doing to herself. I tried to reassure her of how good she looked, but whether she took it seriously, I don't know. On the other hand there are other women I know, who I can only admire. Some have reached their sixties, some have reached their seventies, but you wouldn't know it. One of them still has their own business and runs a shop. She has not allowed 'age' to cause her to retire. She still keeps fit regularly, by working out. She still wears make up, as she has always done. Her clothes are still that of a young person, and the last time I saw her she was just back from holiday and had a terrific tan. Mentally, she is still young and probably always will be. Another woman I know who is in her early sixties still keeps very active, goes out regularly horse-riding and is hardly ever in. She looks good physically and has a good social life. She also has a good positive outlook and is very optimistic. Why should she stop doing the things she loves to do? Who invented retirement anyway? Is it really a good idea? Neither of these women would ever dream of referring to themselves as an old age pensioner, no matter what age they were. To give yourself such a negative title would be the equivalent of pressing the self destruct button.

EVERYTHING ADDS UP

There are many things which contribute to the image you have of yourself, regarding the ageing process. Not only do people start referring to themselves as an old age pensioner, but the very act of retirement itself has a major impact on the subconscious mind. They also start using different words. For example, they might say things like, "Now that I've retired, I'll get a free bus pass" which has the connotation of poverty and poor health. Think about it, rich people probably aren't too concerned about getting something for free, and they probably own their own transport. Therefore you probably wouldn't hear them saying that. Your subconscious associates such a statement with poverty and lack, and this has an extremely powerful effect. The problem is that most people are not aware of how the mind works and these indirect and very subtle statements usually go un-noticed. When you consider the following statements, is it any wonder that some people age quicker?

"I'm an old age pensioner now, don't I get any discount?"
"Now that I've retired, I'll get a free bus pass"
"Set goals at my age? You must be joking!"
"I can't wear that! Do you realise what age I am?"
"Keep fit at my age? I'd probably drop dead!"
"I'm too old to sunbathe"

All of these messages to the subconscious have an accumulative effect and provides a very definite goal. What else can our subconscious do except act upon these very definite and vivid messages? Have you ever seen two people who are exactly the same age and wondered why one looks much younger than the other? There has to be a reason for it, because there's a reason for everything. It can only be a result of what has went on in their minds. Probably a result of different attitudes, different words and emotions, different beliefs and behaviour. One might be a kind, loving person with a good sense of humour, while the other might be a pessimist who is filled up with worry, anger or even hatred. One might be a happy person who is constantly smiling, while the other one is constantly moaning and complaining. I'm not saying that is the case, but you don't know what's going on in the workshop of someone's mind. The happy person ends up with a happy face and people are attracted to them, while the pessimist who is always complaining, repels people because they have developed a sour face, due to a negative emotional state.

HUMOUR

Humour is another thing which positively affects our emotional state, and our physical well being. Some people have a lot of it, but sadly, others don't have so much of it. Laughter is one of the best medicines there is, and it's absolutely free. Laughter makes you feel good all over, and increases your body's ability to fight things off. The Bible says "A cheerful heart is good medicine, but a crushed spirit dries up the bones" (Prov 17: 22). The emotion of humour radiates from you and shows in your body language and your face. If you don't feel as upbeat as normal, you can instantly change your emotional state by changing what you focus on. For example, you could start watching one of your favourite comedies, or you could recall some funny moments from the past. A lot of the time, the determining factor of whether a person has humour or not, is focus. One person might see the funny side of something, while another does not. I remember one time when a friend of mine had just made his lunch. He had his meal on a tray and was just walking from the kitchen through to the living room to sit down and eat it. Suddenly someone bumped into him and his whole meal fell onto the carpet and he was left with the empty tray. Within seconds, his two dogs pounced down from their chairs and literally ate his lunch, off the carpet. Within a few more seconds, everything was gone. He made a few remarks which I won't repeat, but he didn't see the funny side of it. Everyone else in the room, including me (I must be honest) had a grin on their face from ear to ear. We were trying hard not to laugh, but failing miserably. Eventually someone burst out laughing and then everybody else started laughing, including him.

Whether we see the funny side of something or not, is usually habit forming. People usually develop an attitude of humour, or they develop an attitude of pessimism when it comes to things like that. Thus, they get a reputation for being a person who is a good laugh, or an old moan. Better to be the former.

LEARN TO LAUGH AT YOURSELF

It's important that we learn to laugh at ourselves when we mess up. At least your emotions will still be positive and it won't affect you as much. It's also good for your self image. It takes a big person to laugh at themselves, but a small person doesn't. I remember when someone was doing a presentation in front of a room full of people. He was standing at the front of the room explaining the presentation, using a flipchart and marker pens. He was obviously quite nervous and was sweating quite a bit. One can only admire people who have the courage to face their fears, but he was constantly having to wipe his face because the room was also quite hot. Suddenly people went from smiling and nodding in agreement, to actually laughing out loud. He couldn't believe what was happening! People were laughing at him out loud! Then someone came up to him and kindly whispered that there was ink all over his face. What had happened was that the ink from the marker pens had gotten all over his hands and when he wiped his forehead, the ink went from his hands onto his face and mixed with the sweat. As a result, his face was multi coloured and he didn't know it. Fortunately he didn't get embarrassed and saw the funny side of it. He actually handled it well and made a joke out of it. The laughter released a lot of tension in the room and the atmosphere in the room actually became more positively charged, as a result of that. But suppose he had gotten embarrassed and refused to come back up and speak? That could have been the end of him speaking in public. But instead, he saw the humorous side of it, and it became a springboard to his personal development. How you handle things, has an effect on your self image, your inner voice, and will ultimately determine how far you go in life.

MUSIC

The music we listen to also affects our emotional state, and can instantly change our state of mind. Music also brings back memories from the past, some of which are happy, others not so happy. Once again, we are in control of what we listen to, and therefore our emotional state. Music can make us happy or it can make us sad. Depending on what kind of music it is, it could even put you in an aggressive state of mind. If certain music causes you to experience negative emotions such as sadness, self pity, or even aggression, then it can be classed as negative music. But if music causes you to feel uplifted and think happy thoughts, then it is most certainly positive music. Remember that if your thoughts or memories are negative, then you will experience negative emotions. Why do that to yourself when you could just as easily listen to something which will uplift you? It might be worth going back to the list of positive and negative emotions and seeing what emotions the music causes you to feel.

There are certain records that I will never listen to again in my life because my subconscious has somehow made the connection between that piece of music and an extremely negative event in my life that I don't want to dig up. Even though the actual piece of music is good, the memory associated with it is negative and this has the most effect on your mental and emotional state. On the other hand, there are records I love because of the memories associated with them.

Once the subconscious has made a connection like that, it is very difficult to get it to change. I'm not saying it can't be done, but it wouldn't be easy. Sometimes it is just easier to avoid that particular piece of music.

I once tried an experiment to prove that a subconscious connection can be made if we so desire. I decided to make a connection between a piece of film, which involved fighter aircraft and a certain record. What I done was I started playing the archive footage on TV with the sound turned down and played the record at the same time. I watched the footage intensely for the duration of the record, which was probably about four or five minutes. I found that the connection my subconscious made was very powerful indeed. At the time of this writing, the experiment was done over ten years ago and I only done it once. But even today, whenever I hear that record, the images of those planes in combat over the Pacific, still come to mind automatically, whenever I hear that record. Awesome is the power of the subconscious. Awesome is the power of association.

If music causes you to remember a sad event from the past, you will experience the emotion of sadness, even though the actual event has long passed. Likewise, a piece of music might cause you to remember someone you love, or a beautiful time in your life that you spent with this person. In that case you will probably love that record because of the memory associated with it. You can therefore 're-live' that moment mentally, any-time you choose, simply by listening to the record.

We also need to be aware of the words in records. Some music has negative lyrics, while others are packed with words of love and other positive meanings. The danger with negative lyrics, you might find surprising, is singing along. Remember that words are affirmations and your subconscious makes no distinction between singing along to a record, or words that you really mean. It acts upon all words regardless if you mean them or not. Therefore, if you are singing along to a record with negative words, you could be programming yourself to be un-happy. Whereas, if you are singing along to a happy uplifting record, with positive words, you will probably feel even hap-pier, as a result. Whatever thoughts the records make you think, if listened to repeatedly, will become a permanent way of thinking, unless you break the cycle. Most of us probably listen to records every day and the key to impressing something on our subconscious is repetition. Emotion is also a powerful factor, but when the two are combined, the impact is huge. Our sub-conscious is a creature of habit and when we get into the habit of thinking a certain way, it is so easy to keep thinking the same certain way. Sometimes this can also be due to laziness, because it takes effort to break out of a habit and do something new.

I remember listening to a certain record that I had not heard for many years which reminded me of a certain person. Imme-diately upon hearing it, that person and specific time in my life sprung to mind. But the point I want to make is this ; before I heard that record, this person couldn't have been further away from my thoughts. I had absolutely no reason to be thinking about them. So why did I get the thought? I got it because of a process which took place subconsciously. Years ago my subconscious made the association between the person and the record. My subconscious immediately recognised this and sent the information up to my conscious mind in a fraction of a second. So why did that happen? Probably because years ago, when that person was in my life, that record was also a big hit in the charts and it reminded me of that person. It was also a very emotionally charged time in my life. The strangest part of all was that this person had been out of my life for a long time, and I hadn't seen them for at least ten years. After a few days of listening to this record, I suddenly bumped into this person. Was it just coincidence, or was it because of the law of attraction, which states that our most dominant thoughts become manifested in actual physical reality? I believe it was the latter, because similar experiences have occurred too many times in my life to be coincidence. The lesson to be learned? Watch what you allow into your subconscious. It might come true! Our subconscious is very impressionable when in periods of intense emotion. Although the conscious mind may forget, the subconscious never forgets.

The subconscious ability to recall such things in an instant, (without effort) proves that each and every one of us, including you, has a perfect memory. If you are already saying to yourself "That doesn't apply to me, my memory is terrible", then that is part of your problem. You are limiting yourself with negative words and you are actually programming yourself to forget. There's nothing wrong with your memory. You may limit it or cause it to perform badly through the use of negative words or because of negative emotions, but there is still nothing wrong with your memory. Some people cloud their minds with all kinds of negative junk, which makes it extremely difficult for their subconscious to perform well. They then wonder why they have a hard time remembering things and blame the memory itself. It is always our conscious thinking (which provides for the subconscious) which causes our problems. We choose to speak negative words. We choose to think negative thoughts.

We choose to limit ourselves. We choose to allow negative material into our minds. Work on changing your thinking and your words. The same subconscious mind would operate perfectly if given different instructions.

FRIDGE MAGNETS, BUMPER STICKERS AND
OTHER 'INNOCENT' SLOGANS

As already mentioned in the first chapter, everything which is absorbed through your five senses, on a regular basis, makes an impression on your subconscious mind. This is especially true of the written word. It makes no difference what form it's in. It could be a fridge magnet, a poster on your wall, a mug, a key ring, a T-shirt, or even a picture. It's all the same to your subconscious mind. Just the fact that it's in written form, is all that matters. Remember, it makes no difference whatsoever if it is meant to be humorous or some kind of joke, you're subconscious takes everything literally, and looks upon it as a goal to achieve. So the question to ask yourself is "Would I like this to literally become a reality?"

If the answer is 'No' then it's negative. Don't buy it! When something is continually absorbed by your five senses, it becomes part of your subconscious. This then becomes part of your internal guidance system and your subconscious will start to head in that direction and devise ways of bringing it about. It is when we are in a relaxed state, and 'not trying' to take things in, that the subconscious is the most impressionable. For example, if there was a certain advertisement which you passed every day, going to and from work, this advertisement would eventually be firmly embedded in your subconscious mind. Although it might be relatively unimportant, you may find the thought coming into your consciousness once in a while, without knowing where it came from. This is an example of "what is impressed will be expressed".

Some things can be classed as relatively neutral, such as a shop sign because it is neither negative nor positive, it's just 'there'. In fact, you may know it off by heart, simply because your subconscious has absorbed it. But, if for example, you own the merchandise with the slogan on it, or you created a tattoo (which belongs to you) it then affects your self image, because you know it's yours. Let me give you an example. If someone you know has a tattoo which has swear words on it and you see them every day and you see their tattoo every day, it will still be absorbed by your subconscious mind, but it won't have a negative effect on your self image because you know it isn't yours. It would matter, however, if it was your tattoo because since you own it, it becomes part of 'your' self image and affects your emotions. Similarly, if you are in the presence of someone who constantly swears, you may not like to hear it, but at least it won't affect your self image or your emotional state. It will, however affect them far more than it does you, because it's their words.

If you have pictures hanging on your wall or anything in written form, whether at home, or at your workplace, they are all part of your subconscious mind, because you see them regularly. If you have fridge magnets with sayings on them, bumper stickers on your car, or even a tattoo, they are all part of your subconscious mind. Remember, you don't have to be consciously thinking about something in order for it to be operating subconsciously. That's what subconscious means; below the level of consciousness. There is so much going on beneath the surface of consciousness, that there's no way on earth that we could consciously know it all. The wheels of the subconscious are ticking away constantly beneath the surface, by responding emotionally to the goals you have set for it and seeking to make it a reality.

Not only do you need to ask yourself "Is this what I want?" you also need to be aware of the emotions it may be creating. If you have a slogan which 'jokingly' makes fun of another country, not only is it negative, it will cause the emotion of hatred. This programme will then be constantly playing, in the depths of your consciousness. If you have a flag which you believe represents hatred towards another race, this will cause you to suffer from the emotion of hatred and you will not be happy. Football colours can often fall into this category too. It doesn't matter what you want to believe, its what you 'really' believe that affects your subconscious mind. Ask yourself what you truly believe about it, and then act accordingly. But sometimes we ignore our subconscious and our emotions because we consciously want to have something. This is when we make the fatal mistake of thinking we are wiser than our subconscious and we end up setting a negative goal for ourselves and creating a negative emotional state.

For example, I once saw a bumper sticker which said "Worlds Worst Driver" Now that person was probably a nice enough person with a good sense of humour, but they unknowingly set an extremely negative goal for themselves. Subconsciously they set a standard for themselves to live up to. And they shouldn't be surprised if they find themselves living up to it. After all, it is the subconscious which controls about 90 percent of our conditioned responses. Once a person has learned a habit, such as driving, most of it is done subconsciously. The amazing thing is, it's just as easy to set a positive goal, so why not do that instead?

Nowadays you can walk into a shop and buy merchandise with all kinds of slogans on them. Some are relatively 'neutral' such as clothing with the brand name. Very rarely have I seen anything positive. For some strange reason, it seems to be more fashionable if its negative. I remember seeing a fridge magnet in someone's house which said "Dull women have flashy cars" and she had a flashy car! So what did that say about her? Indirectly she was telling herself that she was dull. Was she really dull? I don't think so. Did she want to become dull? I highly doubt it. But she had unknowingly set a goal for her subconscious to live up to. And if she wasn't dull just now, she had just given permission to her subconscious to make her dull. The truth is, we are always in the process of creating the goals we have set for ourselves. We will do things, often without thinking or knowing why, in order to bring about the fulfilment of these goals. This is the subconscious way of making it a reality. Very subtle but extremely powerful. And usually very gradual.

I remember seeing a large poster on someone's bedroom wall which said "I HATE MONDAYS" Would it come as a surprise if that person did actually hate Mondays and dreaded getting up **on Monday morning? It wouldn't surprise me at all** because as long as that poster was up there, it would be an extremely powerful programme in their subconscious mind. If they were to take the poster down and put it out of sight, it would instantly change their state of mind. The point I am trying to make is that the poster was not doing them any good mentally because it was destroying their happiness by replacing it with hatred. As long as they are telling themselves that they hate, then they will hate. The amazing thing is that the person who has the poster on their wall is also affected by it even when **they're not at home. As long as they believe it's** up there (on the wall) then it will operating at a subconscious level and having an effect on them. By now you might be thinking, alright wise guy, suppose they were out somewhere and while they were out, someone took the poster down without them knowing, would it **still affect them? It depends on their beliefs. If they didn't know** it had been taken down and still believed it was up there, then it would still be operating as a subconscious programme. Remember, the subconscious creates according to belief, not according to facts. Some people might argue that the person hated Mondays before they even put the poster up. Well that might be true, but as long as the poster is up there, they always will hate Mondays and will probably never change their attitude. It would be virtually impossible for them to change their attitude and start liking Mondays while that poster was up there. Why? Because the subconscious is more powerful than the conscious. Emotions are subconscious and changing our attitude is a **'conscious' decision. Therefore, the emotions created by the** poster (such as hatred) will over-ride everything else. If that person wanted to hate Mondays, then **there's** no problem, but if they wanted to be happy, then there is a problem because happiness cannot co-exist alongside hatred. One or the other must dominate.

If that person wanted to be happy on a Monday, they could have chosen to take the poster down, throw it in the bin and start **telling themselves that they like Mondays. Even a 'neutral'** picture would be better than a negative poster. They could then start using an affirmation such as "I love Mondays as much as any other day. Every day is exciting for me!" (which is what they want) If for example, they told themselves that they loved Mondays, even when they didn't, subconsciously their mind would start looking for reasons to love Mondays. In other words, their attitude would start to change. But while that poster was up there, their subconscious would be constantly looking for reasons to hate Mondays, and rest assured, it would find them.

I am reminded of the story of the man who fraudulently claimed to be disabled in order to claim government benefits. His love for money was so great that he was willing to go to any lengths to get it. Unknowingly he had set an extremely negative goal for himself, by saying that he was disabled. Even although your subconscious recognises something isn't true just now, it says to itself, "That's my command, so I had better go to work to make it true" It may take a long time to bring it about, or you may even die before it accomplishes it, but rest assured it is working on it day and night and won't give up. He even got a sticker for the back window of his car, to enable him to get privileged parking. Often in the course of conversation he would say "I'm disabled now". Maybe if he could convince enough other people that he was disabled, he might start to believe his own lies and feel 'justified' in claiming the benefits. But if you were to ask him "What's more important to you? Your health or money? Your health or parking spaces?" He would probably reply that his health was far more important. Yet his actions proved otherwise. Actions make a bigger impact on your subconscious than words. Don't get me wrong, words are immensely powerful, but if your words and actions don't add up, your actions are what your subconscious will accept and act upon. In this case, being disabled was the 'goal' behind the actions, which is what the subconscious would accept and act upon. It wouldn't matter one bit, if he said that his health was more important because his actions contradicted his words. Remember, actions speak louder than words, especially to your subconscious.

Just the fact that something is in written form makes a

powerful impact on your subconscious mind, such as the sticker on his back window. This is the negative equivalent to setting a positive goal to achieve your dreams. Why do something as crazy as that? Isn't your health far more important? Think about it this way, if there were no financial benefits involved, would you set a goal for yourself to become disabled? I doubt it. I don't know about you, but my health is far more important to me than any amount of money. The Bible says "For the love of money is a root of all kinds of evil" (1 Tim 6 : 10) and unfortunately it is very true in today's society. We see people making up stories about other people in order to win compensation, when in actual fact it is based on lies. Such people may think they have won, but in actual fact they have lost. They have lost their happiness because 'greed' will be the dominant emotion in their subconscious mind, making happiness impossible. Any time you put money before people, or before God, you will not be happy. In fact, you will be extremely unhappy. They will have lost their peace of mind and also their integrity. I also believe many politicians are unhappy (but not all of them) because many of them put power, money and their own selfish ambitions before what the people want, and also before what's right in the eyes of God. Such people will forsake happiness, by replacing it with the emotions of lust and greed. Although they might be deceived into thinking they are happy, it will elude them. Get your priorities right, and then your world will be right. Then, and only then will you be happy.

YOUR CLOTHES, AND YOUR APPEARANCE

The clothes you wear also affect you at a subconscious level, and influences how you feel about yourself. You can actually make yourself feel better by dressing smarter. You can make yourself feel more confident by acting confidently. You can make yourself feel professional by dressing like a professional. You can make yourself feel more attractive by dressing more attractively. Although the person underneath is still the same, your inner voice changes according to your appearance. Subconsciously we tell ourselves what we think we are.

Have you ever showed up somewhere, or been invited to something, and felt out of your depth because you weren't dressed right? A simple change of clothes might have made all the difference to how you felt. How do you feel when everyone else is wearing suits and ties, and you show up wearing casual gear? While it's true that you may have favourite items of clothing and feel happier wearing certain clothes, your beliefs also play a part. For example, if you believed that a certain type of jacket was worn only by crooks, then no matter how honest you are, if you were to wear one of those jackets, then subconsciously you would 'feel like' a crook. Your inner voice would suddenly change to "I look like a crook" or "Everybody thinks I'm a crook" And as a result of this, you would feel like a crook. Why? Because that is what you believe. It wouldn't matter what you 'consciously' thought because your subconscious is more powerful. Remember, your subconscious creates according to belief. Likewise, if you believe that only professional people wear suits, then every time you wore a suit, you would feel like a professional, because that is also what you believe.

Why not get a new hairstyle or do your hair a different way? Get yourself a new outfit or suit. You might not think small things matter, but they do. A lot of small things combined, make a big difference. Are your shoes shined? Do you smell nice? Everyone loves to smell a pleasant aroma from the opposite sex. Do you look sharp? Or do you look as though you've just been dragged through a hedge backwards? I remember one night when I needed to go out to get petrol. It was late at night and the petrol station was only two minutes round the corner. I was what you might say, slovenly dressed. The jogging bottoms I was wearing had paint marks all over them because I had been painting the house. The top I was wearing was an old jersey which was really only suitable for working in. I was also wearing an old pair of training shoes. I didn't see the point of getting changed, especially when the petrol station was so close. I thought to myself "There probably won't be anyone else there at this time anyway, except the cashier" But part of me also thought "You should really get changed because you are still going to a public place. You will feel better if you do" But I didn't bother to get changed and went out to get petrol. When I got there, there was only one other car. Suddenly the door opened and this girl got out whom I had not seen for years. She was very attractive and I had always thought highly of her. I was delighted to see her, but you can imagine how I regretted not getting changed, but it was too late. Why not dress smart all the time? You never know when you might come across someone you want to impress.

CHAPTER 4

THINK LIKE A SUCCESSFUL PERSON

The difference between successful people and average people, is that successful people control what they allow into their minds. Average people don't do that, and are usually not even aware of the effect that certain input has on our minds. Average people might equate success or failure, to either 'good luck' or 'bad luck' but actually there is no such thing as luck. Why? Because there is a reason for everything. There is such a thing as the law of 'cause and effect'. Everything we do, every action we take, however big or small, has a corresponding effect. What appears to be 'luck' is actually the law of cause and effect, in action. Luck is usually a loser's excuse for not performing. Every situation, outcome, result or event, happens for a reason. If you take a look behind the scenes of a successful person, you will find hard work, sacrifice, commitment, a positive attitude, self control, and a certain plan of action. Take a look behind the scenes of an average person and you often find no plan of action, no dreams or goals, negative words, TV and newspapers are the focus, instead of positive thinking books. Alcohol often plays a part in their lives, and work is often looked upon as something to be dreaded. This is the 'cause' and their lack of achievement is the 'effect'. I once seen a T-shirt which, although was funny, summed up this attitude. It said "Work is the Scourge of the Drinking Class".

The first step in breaking out of failure thinking, into success thinking is awareness. You need to stop, take a look around you and think "Where am I in relation to what my dreams are?" You need to become aware that if what you have been doing up until now is not getting you the results you want in life, it probably never will. I'm sorry if that sounds a bit blunt, but its true. If you don't change, then not much else will. Remember that the height of insanity is to keep doing the same thing over and over, while expecting different results. I can honestly tell you that I used to think that way myself. I was in a failure mode of thinking for years, with failure habits. But I wasn't prepared to change. I thought that if I kept on doing what I was doing long enough, eventually I would make a breakthrough and life would suddenly improve.

I was wrong. The breakthrough never came and I was cruelly disillusioned. I wasted years in the failure mode, when, if only I had been aware, could have began to take control, by changing my thinking. I don't want you to fall into the same trap. If you are quite happy with your results in life, that's fine, but if not, then something has to change and that 'something' is YOU. Once you become aware, the next step is to take action. Successful people know that whatever you allow into your subconscious controls your life. Therefore they are very select in what they read, what they listen to, and who they hang around with. These three things, more than anything else, will determine where you end up in life. They will determine your happiness, your self image, your level of achievements, your level of confidence, the quality of your relationships, your level of income and your beliefs. I have covered these things in more detail in my other book, "You Are The Problem, You Are The Solution" but because they are so vitally important, I will list them again here:

WHAT YOU READ
WHAT YOU LISTEN TO
WHO YOU ASSOCIATE WITH

If you decide to take control of your life by changing these three things, your life will start to go in a whole new direction and life will take on a whole new meaning. Make them a habit and you will never look back because of the benefits which come from them. Let's take a look at each one:

WHAT YOU READ

Make it a habit to read from a positive thinking book for fifteen minutes every day. Where do you get the time to do that? Quit reading newspapers and start reading something which will create positive emotions instead. This will contribute enormously to your own personal development. At your local bookstore, you will find a great selection under 'self help'. Some recommended titles and authors include:

The Magic of Thinking Big (David J Schwartz)

How to Win Friends and Influence People (Dale Carnegie)

How to Stop Worrying and Start Living (Dale Carnegie)

Rich Dad, Poor Dad (Robert Kiyosaki)

Cashflow Quadrant (Robert Kiyosaki)

Psycho Cybernetics (Maxwell Maltz)

Think and Grow Rich (Napoleon Hill)

Become a Better You (Joel Osteen)

The Power of Your Subconscious Mind (Dr. Joseph Murphy)

What to Say When You Talk to Yourself (Shad Helmstetter)

Body Language (Allan Pease)

When you read, you also talk silently to yourself, which re-directs your inner voice. Reading replaces faulty beliefs with the truth. It destroys self imposed limitations and builds self confidence. If you are suffering from a poor self image, or have had negative experiences in the past, reading will eventually over-ride and replace any negative beliefs you have about yourself. I think its sad that none of these books are taught in schools. Maybe things have changed since I was at school, but in all the years I spent at school, we never had one single positive thinking book. Neither was anything ever taught about the importance of a positive mental attitude. Some of the most fundamental success habits are simply not taught. Why? In my opinion, it is because the whole of the school system is geared towards teaching people to be average. They are taught to get a job instead of being a business owner. They are taught to think small instead of thinking big. As a result of 'average thinking' most people often work hard their whole lives without coming anywhere near achieving their dreams. Then they retire, often disillusioned and cynical towards life. Average thinking produces average results. Thinking big produces big results. As David Schwartz explains in 'The Magic of Thinking Big' most people who are high achievers in life are not any smarter than anyone else, the difference is, they think far bigger. Thinking always comes first, then actions, then results. Take control of your life by taking control of your thinking.

WHAT YOU LISTEN TO

Most people turn on the TV or radio out of sheer habit. Why not leave the TV and radio off, and replace it by listening to motivational CD's instead? Many of the famous authors have websites which you can also order CD's from. What you listen to repeatedly becomes your focus in life. What you focus on continually, is what you attract. Let me illustrate; If you were cutting a piece of wood with a saw, you could either focus on one of two things. You could focus on successfully cutting through the wood, or you could visualise yourself making a mistake and cutting yourself. It's when you start thinking about what you don't want, (making a mistake) that you end up cutting yourself. Why? Because you attract what you focus on, even if you don't want that to happen. Your subconscious always goes in the direction of what you focus on because that's its goal. You have a far higher chance of successfully cutting through the wood if you focus only on doing it right. Keep what you don't want, out of your mind. Focus only on what you do want.

In the same way, many people continually focus on what they don't want, by listening to the radio and the news every day. Every hour you can hear about violent crime, car crashes and all sorts of negative things. Why focus on that if you don't want that? Listening to it doesn't help the victim and it doesn't help you either, so why do it? It will only depress you by filling your mind with negative emotions. And how close will this bring you to your dreams? It will actually take you further away. I've known people to suddenly fly into a rage, as a result of something they heard on the radio, or saw on TV. Why punish yourself like that? Why not let your dreams become your focus (which is what you want) Why not listen to people talking about success instead? You'll certainly be a lot happier. Your emotions will be far more positive and you will be heading in the direction of your dreams. The chances are, you probably spend a lot of your time in your car driving to and from work. Why not use this time as an opportunity to learn, as well as motivating yourself? Turn your car into a 'university on wheels'. You might find you enjoy the journey much more!

WHO YOU ASSOCIATE WITH

Choose your associates carefully. Whether we like it or not, we become like the people we associate with. Often we develop our habits and attitudes from the people we spend the most time with. Do they speak positively or negatively? Do they have integrity? Are they ambitious or are they always looking for something for nothing? Are they actively pursuing their dreams and goals? More importantly, do they have any? Do they spend their time wisely, or do they waste it in front of the TV? If you want to be where they are in life, then associate with them. If not then it might be an idea to find some new friends. By attending seminars, you will have an opportunity to meet new friends, learn new things and learn how to create wealth. This can help take your life to a whole new level.

Have you ever heard the sayings ; "Birds of a feather flock together" and "Show me who your friends are, and I'll tell you who you are" Well, there is a lot of truth in that. I once heard an extremely successful business owner giving a talk to a group of people. He asked them all to write down their five closest friends or associates, currently in their lives. Then he said, "You are looking at your future". He went on to say "The chances are, your level of income will probably be about the average of your five closest friends. Rarely does it ever rise above that".

It's sad but true, that many people, or so called 'friends' don't want you to get ahead of them. If they think you are on to something which could put you ahead of them financially, often they will try and discourage you. It could be because of jealousy, or it could be because they are afraid to do something themselves. They may criticise you and tell you it won't work, or that you don't have what it takes to succeed. That's not a friend! A true friend will support you, not discourage you. If you want to succeed, you need to cut loose from people like that, otherwise they will sabotage your success. I can tell you from personal experience that the same thing happened to me when I got involved in multi-level marketing. I had a 'friend' who kept telling me it was no good, and kept reminding me of all the reasons why it wouldn't work. He was wrong, because if I hadn't got involved in MLM, you wouldn't be reading this book just now. I realised very quickly that it was going to be impossible to succeed while I was associating with him, so I had to cut loose. Don't get me wrong, we are still good friends, but I just don't associate with him anymore. Since then, I have gained a lot more 'true friends'. I have met many extremely successful people, through going to business seminars. I met people who looked for reasons why something would work, rather than reasons why it wouldn't. They were people who were not only interested in making money, but were also interested in me, as a person. They encouraged me, they listened when I had problems and they bent over backwards to help me. They even helped me when it was of no personal benefit to themselves. That's a true friend!

It's also a sad fact today that many young people get involved in crime. The saddest part to me, is that it's so un-necessary. Every one of these people who commit serious crimes, have the potential to become great. They just choose not to. They have as much potential as you and me, only they refuse to believe it. Had they made different choices and associated with different people they might have become successful. Instead, they simply choose the negative path instead of the positive. When someone commits' a crime, although it is wrong and often downright evil, it does not take away from their potential. If they wanted to change, they could. Their potential is still there, and always will be. It's just that they turn their back on it and refuse to recognise it. They refuse to recognise the greatness God has put inside of them. I cannot stress enough, the importance of associating with the right people. It will determine where you end up in life. If they are negative, you will become negative. If they talk about being broke all the time, there's a good chance you will end up broke. If they have no goals or dreams, and you do, they will probably steal yours. But if you associate with positive people, who are going somewhere in life, there's a good chance they can help you to do the same. Why not choose success? You have the potential inside of you.

LIFE IS GEARED TO DRAG YOU DOWN

That's not supposed to be a negative statement, but we need to realise that life is a battle, and it is a fight to stay positive and a fight to succeed. We do not have to try to be negative, and we do not have to try to fail. It will happen automatically if we fail to discipline ourselves and fail to take control of what goes into our minds. Someone once said, and I believe it is true, "If you fail to plan, then you are really planning to fail". When you decide to change direction and embark on a journey towards your dreams, or even a journey of self improvement, realise that you are doing what 95 percent of the population are not willing to do. Therefore you are going to encounter opposition. Some of it may even be quite fierce at times. You may be looked upon as 'different' or even some kind of odd ball. But don't worry about it. You are the one who is going to reap the rewards. Einstein said "Great thinkers have always encountered violent opposition from mediocre minds". General Patton who commanded US forces in World War Two said "If everyone is thinking alike, no-one is really thinking". Therefore, if you want to win at the game of life, you need to think outside the box. Just for a moment, imagine you are a fish swimming downstream. Suddenly you about-turn and start heading upstream. Everything is suddenly against you. The current is against you, it takes much more effort and you are vastly outnumbered because 95 percent of the fish are swimming past you, in the opposite direction. They barge into you, obstruct you and cause you all kinds of hardship. Therefore, adversity and opposition are to be expected. Well, it's the same in life. Don't expect to embark on a journey towards your dreams, without opposition. Remember that 95 percent of the population are living in the comfort zone and are not willing to step out, let alone pursue their dreams. Therefore, they will barge into you, obstruct you and cause you all kinds of hardship.

The forces in life are sent against us to try and keep us broke or average at best. I have already mentioned that the school system is designed to keep people average. We come across people who laugh at our ideas and tell us they won't work. We encounter criticism and ridicule from people who don't want us to get ahead of them. Newspapers and TV pollute our minds with negative thoughts which cause negative emotions, such as worry, doubt, anger and fear. We are bombarded with things which tempt us, such as pornography. We are also bombarded with advertisements encouraging us to get into debt for things we usually don't need. If you want to become broke, getting into credit card debt is probably one of the fastest ways to get there. The loan sharks couldn't care less what happens to you, they only care about making money. Therefore you need to look after yourself. How do you do that? Get educated! Commit to an ongoing personal development programme. Life may be geared to drag you down, but it doesn't have to. It is still possible to rise above it. Life will only drag you down if you let it. But it all begins by taking control of your mind. If you don't, then you are liable to be tossed around here, there and everywhere, by the circumstances of life. Earl Nightingale likens it to a ship without a rudder. And when you have no direction or goal, then any path will do. Unfortunately that's what happens to most people. They may be getting by, but they have no definite dreams or purpose. As a result, they just drift aimlessly through life.

BUT IT DOESN'T HAVE TO BE THAT WAY

But you can, if you choose, set some goals and focus on your dreams. You can if you wish, put a plan into action and actively work towards pursuing your dreams. You can if you choose, replace failure habits with success habits. You can also choose to get educated. Success is a choice, and so is failure. When you finish reading these words, you have a choice; you can watch TV or you can take some sort of action towards the achievement of your dreams. Why not call on a new prospect? Why not get out of your house and meet some new people? Why not go and view one of your dream homes and get a picture of it? Why not test drive your dream car? Why not go down to the travel agent and get a brochure of one of your favourite holiday resorts? Why not get in touch with one of your favourite charities and set a goal to do something for humanity? It's your choice!

I remember hearing a veteran fighter pilot talking about how he thought about his destiny. He served in World War Two, and flew Hellcats from aircraft carriers in the Pacific. He made many kills, in dogfights with the Japanese. His exact words were ; "There's no script yet that says you're going to get killed tomorrow. If you're smart enough, if you're sharp enough, you can control your own destiny".

YOU ARE VALUABLE

Unfortunately, most people sell themselves short. Adults are actually far worse (or should I say better?) at this than children. Why? Because life has knocked the confidence out of them. The more time that has passed by, the longer they've had to develop false beliefs and become cynical. The more negative experiences they've had, the longer they've had to develop a poor self image. They've had more time to tell themselves why they don't believe in themselves and that they probably won't achieve their dreams, so they may as well forget about it. I know this isn't the case for everyone, but sadly it is for many people

A person with a lot of self confidence is not any more valuable than a person with a poor self image. A person who has achieved a high level of success in life, is not any more valuable than a person with an inferiority complex. Every human being, whether they are rich or poor, tall or short, fat or skinny, confident or lacking confidence is equally as valuable, and equally important to God. Our value, as human beings cannot be taken away. If a person believes they are totally worthless, it is only because of false beliefs and nothing to do with the truth. It doesn't matter what you believe about yourself, your potential and your value cannot be taken away. Why? Because when God created you, He equipped you with absolutely everything you need in order to be extremely successful. But as we get older, life and other people knock it out of us. Knock what out of us? Confidence and self belief, but certainly not value. Let me give you an example; suppose I take a pound coin out of my pocket and decide to treat it badly. I throw it as far as I can, then I pick it up, bounce it off every wall, as hard as I can. Then I walk right over it and kick it around. I spit on it and then I shout all kinds of abuse at it. What's it worth now? Still one pound! Although it might look dirty and unclean, its value is unaffected. Well, it's the same with us. We may have experienced similar things in the past, but our value is still the same, and always will be. The difference between us and the coin is that we have a belief system. Although our value is not affected, our beliefs are. And that is the danger. Remember, if you believe it, then it's true for you. When your beliefs are affected, your self-image is affected. This then affects your emotional state (such as happiness) and also your confidence level. This might sound crazy, but its true; It is possible to believe you are worthless, when you are valuable. Once again, it is all to do with beliefs. The value doesn't change, only beliefs. The person who believes they are valuable has a good, realistic self-image, which is based on truth. They appreciate their God given abilities and make full use of them. But a person who believes they are worthless, when they are actually valuable, does not realise the potential they have within them. It's not that the potential isn't there, it simply lies dormant and unused. As a result, they sell themselves short and live an average life at best. What a waste of potential! Don't you want to make as much use of your potential as possible! I know that I do!

THE GOOD NEWS

Wouldn't it be terrible if we were already at our full potential and unable to change? If that was true, there would be a lot of hopeless people walking about, because there would be no prospect of having a better life. But the good news is that even if you believe negative things about yourself, they can be changed. There is nothing in your past, which needs to have any control over your future. A fresh start is always possible for any human being. It may be a long hard road to recovery, but the door is always open and always will be. The possibility for change is always there. The person who feels totally defeated and worthless today could be the same person who ends up inspiring thousands of people from an auditorium one day. I have seen this happen so many times, it's amazing. Many of the greatest motivational speakers I have heard talk, were at some point in their lives, afraid to get up in front of a few people and say their name. That was certainly true of me. Therefore they must have had the potential all along, or it would not have been possible to change. Yet if you were to go back a few years, many of them might not have believed they had the potential. This is exactly what keeps the vast majority of people from succeeding in life. False beliefs. These false beliefs are then lived out, as though they were true and we limit ourselves and tell ourselves we are not capable. I have heard motivational speakers, who are extremely wealthy today, say that when they were showing a presentation in someone's house, they would often go to the bathroom first and be physically sick because of fear. Yet they became successful because they persisted in spite of their fears. Fear affects all of us in different ways. My greatest fear was that I would walk on to the stage and the words wouldn't come out, because of fear. I know that God was certainly helping me at those times. Although I felt I came close to it happening, it never actually happened. The Bible says "When you pass through the waters, I will be with you" (Isa 43: 2) But the important thing is that you face your fear, because when you face it, you begin to destroy fear. Each time you do what you fear, the fear gets smaller and your self confidence increases. But if you avoid doing what you fear, the fear gets bigger. You need to destroy fear before it destroys you.

Although I am not a motivational speaker (yet!), I have spoken a few times in public, and I will be honest enough to say that the initial fear of getting up in front of a room full of people and saying my name was tremendous. It was so bad that it almost stopped me in my tracks. Without the help of positive thinking books, positive affirmations and more importantly, the help of the Almighty, I could not have done it. God has worked miracles in my life, and He will do the same for you, but you need to ask Him. You need to include Him in your life. Trying to do something by yourself is trying to do it the hard way. Why not ask for help?

The only way to overcome your fears is to continually expose yourself to them. The more exposure you get, the less of a grip fear will have on you. Slowly you begin to master fear, instead of having it master you. Think about it another way, it is impossible to master something if you avoid it. You need to be in contact with something if you are to stand any chance of defeating it. How could an army possibly defeat another army if they didn't engage them on the battlefield? They certainly wouldn't defeat them by avoiding them. Take opportunities to confront your fears when they arise. Volunteer to speak if you get the chance, even if it is only at a small family gathering. All the little opportunities are far more important than you think, because all the little experiences put together contribute to your overall self image and make you who you are.

SUCCESS BREEDS SUCCESS

You may think that relatively small opportunities to face your fears are unimportant, but this is a huge mistake. Each 'small opportunity' is still a step forward from where you used to be. The size of the step doesn't matter. The only thing that matters is the direction in which you go. There are only two directions, you are either facing your fears or you are running from them. Let me give you an example; suppose you have a fear of speaking in public and you get an opportunity to say a few words on the microphone at one of your relative's birthday party. You may be tempted to think "I don't like public speaking anyway. It's just a silly little party. I'll simply decline and say I can't make it." As a result, you miss out on an opportunity to take a step forward, gain some experience and increase your self confidence. (The key word in that sentence is 'forward' because it denotes the direction, which is toward fear) It may have seemed like a small little opportunity that you declined to take, but by declining, you have actually taken a step backwards.

What do you think happens when you are faced with a bigger opportunity later on? This time it may be a little bit bigger in terms of fear. It might mean speaking in front of a bigger group, where you hardly know anyone. Well, had you taken the previous opportunity, you would have gained some self confidence and you would have felt better about facing something a little bit bigger. But because you declined, you actually lost confidence, and now the fear is much bigger than before, all because you took a small step backwards at the 'little opportunity' When you take a little step backwards at the little opportunity, it causes you to take big steps backwards at the big opportunities. And on the cycle goes, until you decide to make a stand and face it.

But the good news is that even small victories help us to get to the next victory. Success breeds success. If you take every opportunity possible, to face your fears, you will find that your fears begin to lessen. You will also find that you improve a little bit each time. Each time you take action to do the thing you fear, your self image improves and your ability to perform improves. In other words, each success, no matter how small, provides the foundation for the next step. Imagine all the small opportunities are like stepping stones across a river. Now, imagine there are ten stepping stones to get from one side to the other. It would be far too big a jump from the first stone to the tenth. Fear is a bit like that. If you look too far down the road, it can seem overwhelming, but if you take one stepping stone at a time (or one opportunity at a time) eventually you will get to the other side.

The stepping stones change your beliefs. They also change your self image. Ironically, the situations we so often try to avoid are the very building blocks to what we become. Eventually you might even get to a point where you actually enjoy what you once had fear of. I can testify to that myself. I know of many cases where people who originally had tremendous fear of public speaking, persisted and persisted until they got to a point where you couldn't shut them up. If you are afraid, why not use affirmations such as:

"I am strong and courageous".
"I am confident and courageous.
"I can do all things through Christ, who strengthens me".

Eventually you will get to a point where you look back and think "What was I so afraid of?" Often we are afraid of fear itself. Often we are afraid of our own thoughts. Take action, it's the only way to destroy fear.

NATURE SEEKS BALANCE

Did you know that Mother Nature is the great equaliser? This falls in line with Bible teaching, which says "Do not be deceived; God cannot be mocked. A man reaps what he sows" (Gal 6: 7) Not only does this principle hold true regarding our actions and how we treat other people, but in everything we do. If we sow love, we will reap love. If we sow hatred, we will reap hatred. If we sow compliments, we will reap compliments. If we sow criticism, we will reap criticism. If we sow good will, we will reap good will. Every action has a corresponding reaction. Every cause has an effect and every effect has a cause. Nothing happens by chance. There is a reason for everything and usually we have sown the seeds, either knowingly or unknowingly.

There is no such thing as something for nothing because, this would indicate an unbalance. It would mean that you have gained without giving, and Mother Nature will very quickly seek to balance the scales. You might appear to think you have got away with it, but that is exactly why the first four words of the above Bible verse say "Do not be deceived" because the scales have to, and will be made level, in one way or another. If there's an up, there has to be a down. If there's a hot, there must be a cold. If there's a plus, there must be a minus. If there's a positive, there has to be a negative. If there's a heaven, there must be a hell.

Many people in life try to get something for nothing. For example, a bank robber may rob a bank, get away with millions of pounds, flee to another country and think they can enjoy the good life forever more. They have been deceived. They may have money, but they will have sacrificed their peace of mind because they will probably be on the run forever, or until they get caught. They will have sacrificed their happiness and re-placed it with negative emotions such as greed and guilt. As long as they are on the run, which may be forever, these negative emotions, along with fear, and possibly anxiety, will dominate their minds. Is it worth it, just for money? Definitely not! This is probably just part of the great equaliser, in response to appearing to get something for nothing. The perceived 'plus' is equalised with a huge minus. It's not worth it.

A person may cheat, steal, lie and live off government benefits for the rest of their life and be deceived into thinking they have gained without forfeiting anything themselves. They are wrong because their self image will be in the gutter. They will have missed out on opportunities to become wealthy, and will have consigned themselves to life just above the poverty line. They will not have developed any more of their potential, and will probably never achieve their dreams in life. Yet, they may think they've won at the game of life! The great equaliser may affect them without them even realising there is such a thing.

MAKE NO MISTAKE, THE SCALES WILL BE BALANCED

A person who has never had a lot of money, may suddenly win millions on the lottery. Statistics have shown that when this happens, most people experience the downside and end up with a whole bunch of problems, as a result. Initially, they experienced a massive high, but put forth no effort to get it. Therefore, there is a huge unbalance. Then Mother Nature very quickly moves in, to balance the scales. There's nothing wrong with having a massive high, but if that 'high' has been gotten for nothing then there is a huge unbalance. There now has to be a corresponding 'low' because Mother Nature will not sit idly by, while there is any kind of unbalance. Often these people end up broke, or coming to ruin through things such as drugs and alcohol, or sexually immoral behaviour. They might lose many of their friends and possibly their reputation. The great equaliser could even result in death.

But I don't want you to think that there's anything wrong with making money or becoming wealthy. There's not, as long as it is gained honestly and you've had to put forth effort in order to get it. You could say that the effort is equalised by the reward of wealth. Thus, there is a balance. That's why persistence always pays off. You may be involved in some kind of business venture or project, and are putting forth a lot of effort and seeing no immediate reward. But rest assured, nature is seeking to reward your efforts. Personally I prefer to say God is seeking to reward your efforts, after all, He created mother nature. But that is your personal choice. The reward might take a long time. It might be gradual instead of sudden, but the scales will, in the long run, be balanced. I know of many independent business owners who put forth years of effort building their businesses, without seeing any immediate financial reward. Infact, it was quite some time, and also a test of faith before they made any substantial amounts of money. The minus or the 'low' if that's what you want to call it, would probably have been the years of painstaking work, reading books, sacrificing some of their spare time while their friends were out enjoying themselves. During the years of hard work and sacrifice, they were creating a huge unbalance. Not to mention all the rejections they had, and all the ridicule they endured. Yet they persisted. Suddenly, it was as if God had opened the floodgates of heaven, and they were blessed with huge amounts of wealth. Through faith and persistence, they eventually made a breakthrough. Tremendous wealth was the great equaliser for their years of effort. Not only wealth but more importantly, their self image would have improved, as a result of their struggles.

YOU ALWAYS GET BACK MORE THAN YOU GIVE

Not only do we get back what we give, but it also comes back multiplied. For example, if you give some money to charity, the good you reap is always far greater than what you sow. We should not give 'to' get, we should give for the right reasons, but that's how it works. Often it comes back in not so obvious ways. For example, you may give £100 to a charity and God might save you thousands of pounds on the new car you are looking for. He might cause you to get a 'bargain' which 'seems like' coincidence. Understand that you will never be worse off, by giving, because you cannot out-give God. God will always give you back far more than you give. Therefore it makes even more sense to sow what's good. It's just like planting a seed in the ground. The seed you plant is very small, but the flower which comes from it, starts to grow and is much bigger than what you first deposited in the ground. When you do something, whether good or bad, you deposit a seed (a thought) in your mind. These thoughts develop and grow, at a subconscious level, always attracting after their own kind, and grow until they are in full bloom. Eventually you get a harvest and the harvest is always in accordance with the type of seed you have sown. It would be impossible to plant the seed of a flower and expect to get vegetables, or to plant an orange tree and get bananas. Likewise, if you plant evil, you cannot reap anything but evil, and it will come back multiplied. The Bible says "He who sows wickedness reaps trouble" (Prov 22: 8) On the other hand, if you sow kindness, generosity and love, it will also come back multiplied. Your relationships improve, and your very quality of life improves. Therefore, your level of happiness also improves. Whatever you give you will receive, but whatever you are unwilling to give, you will be unable to receive. That's why greed never prospers, because greedy people are unwilling to give. Therefore, they are unable to receive, and end up poor and unhappy. Over and over, the Bible tells us that the righteous will prosper. "Misfortune pursues the sinner, but prosperity is the reward of the righteous" (Prov 13: 21) Therefore, if you are willing to give money, you will open the floodgates and allow God to pour abundance into your life. If not, then His hands are tied. Make no mistake, God wants to give you abundance and He wants you to prosper but you must do it His way, by being generous. "Whoever sows sparingly will also reap sparingly, and whoever sows generously will also reap generously" (2 Cor 9: 6)

THINK BIG

Most people stay average because they think average. It's not that they don't have the capabilities, they do, but the problem is that they think too small. When you think small, you end up with small results and small achievements. Why? Because that's the goal you set for your subconscious to act upon. The goal that you set consciously is what you will aspire to achieve, subconsciously. If you accept that you are only worth a certain amount of money, in terms of a pay-cheque, and that is your 'limit' then don't expect to earn much more than that. Subconsciously you will probably only apply for positions which pay that amount, or less. If for some reason you found yourself 'out of your depth' and had the opportunity of working in a position which paid much more than that, then subconsciously you would self sabotage your success. Subconsciously you would do things to mess it up, or you would find reasons to talk yourself out of it, because the goal you set for yourself was way below that, and no higher.

When you accept something 'consciously' (such as a financial target or a goal, or even something to do with your self-image) your subconscious immediately aligns itself with that goal and goes all out to achieve it. Everything you do, every action you take, every word you speak, every thought you think, from there on, will be subconsciously aligned with achieving that goal. Often you won't even be aware of it, because you will be doing it subconsciously. For example if you have an important exam to pass, you will probably consciously set the goal of passing the exam. You will tell yourself "I must pass that exam" Therefore, your behaviour would automatically line up with that goal. You wouldn't mind sacrificing some evenings in order to study. You would automatically want to have all the appropriate materials to read. You would happily buy whatever was necessary to help you to learn, and you would discipline yourself by allocating a certain amount of time to study. You would probably also picture yourself passing the exam. All this shows how you subconsciously align everything in accordance with the goal you have set for yourself, because your goal is to pass.

But unfortunately some people set goals to reap average results, and they succeed too! Imagine someone telling themselves that they will get a poor result. When they accept that they are going to get a poor result, or even fail, then all their actions will align themselves with getting a poor result, so that they achieve it and they are not disappointed. They would probably find themselves not studying very much and not doing what was required in order to learn. Imagine a football team coming onto the field thinking the other team are superior, or telling themselves that the best they can hope for is a draw. What do you think will happen? They're going to get wiped out! Why? Because they're expecting to. Subconsciously, they have accepted defeat and subconsciously their actions will line up with the goal of getting beat. This will be reflected in how they play, and every action they take. Often this can be a result of poor management.

Thinking small is extremely common. Take the case of Fred. Fred has just got his first book published. It has cost him several thousand pounds to get his book published. Fred is a big thinker, but all his friends think small. Fred is thinking along the lines of a bestseller, selling millions of copies. Therefore all his actions, including the quality of his writing would have aligned themselves with the goal of being a bestseller. Subconsciously he would have been thinking, "This needs to be a good book because its going to sell millions of copies" Therefore all his actions would line up with producing a book which was good enough to be a bestseller. Otherwise he might not try as hard, and just write an 'average book'.

But his friends don't think that way. Instead of focusing on being a bestseller, they are focusing on the amount of money it has cost Fred to get it published. They have figured out that Fred needs to sell a certain amount of copies to break even, so that he re-coups his money and doesn't lose anything. Fred is thinking big but his friends are only thinking about not losing. Subconsciously, their actions would be different, in order to achieve different goals. How can you expect to achieve big, by thinking that small. You can't, and you won't. Now I realise these people mean well and genuinely care about Fred, but they are not helping. Therefore Fred mentally has to shut the doors on that type of thinking and keep in mind the thought (or goal) of being a bestseller.

ARE YOU REALLY HAPPY?

Are you really as happy as you can be? If you answered yes, how do you know? How do you know that you can't be even happier? Is there a limit to happiness? If there was, how would you know you had reached it? And how do you know that you couldn't be happier still? Abraham Lincoln said that "Most people are about as happy as they make up their minds to be" But there's more to it than that, because happiness is a by-product of doing what's right and doing what we enjoy, and also having a positive mental attitude. Therefore, by our actions and thoughts, we decide how happy we will be. We can tell ourselves it's a miserable day outside and that we hate our job, or we can be grateful we are alive and grateful we live in a free, democratic country, with food on the table and a roof over our heads. Therefore happiness, to a large degree, is chosen.

It always amazes me that often, the people who have everything going for them, complain about the most trivial things, such as the weather. Often the people who have everything they need, start to look for perfection, because things are not quite the way they would like them. If the slightest thing irritates them, they start to moan and complain. They start to focus on what they don't have instead of what they do have, they start to focus on little irritating things instead of being grateful for their health, and everything else we take for granted. And before they know it, they are no longer happy. Their negative words created a negative emotional state and made happiness impossible. They forget that there are people in this world who would love to change places with them. Thank goodness we don't live in a Communist country, or a war torn part of the world, or a country riddled with famine and disease. Let's be grateful for what we do have. The Bible says "For this is the day the Lord has made, let us rejoice and be glad in it" (Ps 118: 24). This doesn't mean we should turn a blind eye to other peoples plights. We, as Christians should be doing as much as we can to help them, even though it means sacrificing something ourselves, but at the same time being grateful for what we have.

THE HAPPINESS ILLUSION

Some people may think they are as happy as they can be. They might be addicted to alcohol, drugs and sexually immoral behaviour and think they are at the very pinnacle of happiness. They have been deceived. That's exactly what the devil wants you to think, so that you don't go any higher in life, you don't achieve your dreams, you don't become wealthy, you have a poor self image, and you are ineffective for God. Thus you are enslaved and defeated.

If someone has lived this way for a long time, or for most of their lives then they might not believe it is possible to be happier because they have nothing to compare it to. Therefore they might be content to continue on the path they are on, never ever rising higher, missing opportunities, living without purpose and having no clear-cut dreams or goals. Every day being much the same as the last. They might think that if they were to give up some of these things, they would be far less happy than they are right now. As a result, they stay addicted because they believe they 'need it' in order to be happy. This is one of the greatest lies Satan ever inflicts on us. How do I know? Because I've been there. I've been addicted. I know how Satan can mess up our belief system by convincing us that we can't get by without these things. I know how Satan convinces us that these are essential for our happiness and that we will be miserable without them. The Bible says of the devil "When he lies, he speaks his native language, for he is a liar and the father of lies" (John 8 : 44) The sad part is that many people never ever break free from addictions. Why? In my opinion it is largely due to false beliefs. They are completely convinced that they need them and therefore stay addicted. The battle is more mental than physical. Although the Bible condemns such behaviour, Jesus brings us good news and gives us hope; "The thief comes only to steal and kill and destroy; I have come that they may have life and have it to the full" (John 10: 10)

God wants you to have a life of abundance and live life to the full, but the only way to do that is to obey Him. This means breaking free from the things which are keeping you in bondage. Breaking free from false beliefs, and things which are enslaving you, deceiving you, keeping you broke and keeping you in a negative state of mind. Instead, God wants you to be happy, successful, and to achieve your dreams, to have a good self-image, to rise higher and higher, to become wealthy, to live the abundant life and to have a strong healthy body. But all this cannot be achieved until you break free from these addictions. Why not ask God to help you to break free from the devils grip? "Then they cried to the Lord in their trouble, and He saved them from their distress. He brought them out of darkness and the deepest gloom and broke away their chains" (Ps 107: 13-14)

God wants to give you the desires of your heart, but until

you break free from addictions and start to obey Him, His hands are tied. As we are promised in the Bible; "Delight yourself in the Lord and he will give you the desires of your heart" (Ps 37 : 4)

Imagine for a moment that happiness was measured on a scale from one to ten. Ten being extremely happy and one being extremely unhappy. Where would you place yourself regarding your life in general? Would you rate yourself an eight, a nine or maybe even a ten? Or would it be much lower? Everyone's answer is different. In fact some people who are addicted may even rate themselves a ten. Now imagine that we compared the scale of happiness to the rungs on a ladder.

Even although you might have rated yourself a nine or a ten, you suddenly found out the ladder had hundreds of rungs, which went far higher than rung ten. All the time you believed you were at the maximum level of happiness, you suddenly become aware that it is possible to be far happier than you are right now. You might think to yourself "I just didn't believe the ladder was as high as that! For all my life, I thought that this ladder only had ten rungs. I thought I was at the very pinnacle. I wonder what the view is like higher up? You were deceived into thinking that if you gave up some of these addictions that you might descend even further, possibly to rung one or two. But you realise that not only is this a lie but the ladder is also un-limited in height. And giving up these addictions actually does the opposite and puts you much higher up the ladder instead of lowering you down. How do you feel now? Overjoyed? Happy? Cheated? Confused? Mixed emotions? Obviously this would be a paradigm shift and a revelation to all of us, but that's what often happens when you give up an addiction. It's like chains falling off you. You experience a freedom and peace you have never known before. The reason being; you are on a rung that not only is much higher, but you never knew existed. You look back on the addiction, which once looked so promising, and realise it was actually your prison. Sadly, many people who are in their 'psychological prisons' do not believe they are in such prisons. They are convinced the ladder only has ten rungs and they are at the top of the ladder. But the truth is, the ladder is unlimited in height.

UNLIMITED

If you dispute this, please come back and tell me who has been at the top. Who can claim to be at the top, when they cannot prove that it can go even higher still? And if it can, how would they know until they had been there? An addiction locks you into a certain rung on the ladder, both physically and mentally, and you get stuck there. You find it difficult to move, or you may not even want to move, especially if you think you are at the top. Why would someone want to move if they believe they are already at the top? But when you break free from these addictions, you will rise so much higher up the ladder, that you will look down on rung ten from a great height and think "What a miserable, horrible, dark rung that was! How could I possibly have wanted to stay there? If I had known what it was like up here, I would have left rung ten long ago!" Why not do it now? Why waste another day? A day at rung ten is a day wasted. True happiness is being free from addictions and not being in bondage to them. The Bible says "Then you will know the truth, and the truth will set you free" (John 8 : 32)

MAKING YOUR SUBCONSCIOUS WORK FOR YOU INSTEAD OF AGAINST YOU

I am reminded of the story of a woman who used to nag her husband. Deep down, she didn't really want to nag him, but the problem was that no matter how hard she tried not to, she would always end up nagging him. Through a lack of knowledge of how the mind works, she was actually programming herself to fail, without knowing it. Instead of affirming what she wanted, (which was to get on well with him) she was affirming the opposite of an idea, and it was backfiring on her. She was constantly reminding her subconscious of 'what not to do' instead of 'what to do'.

Let's say her husband's name was Mike. She would regularly say to herself "I must not nag Mike today" or "I'm going to try hard not to moan at Mike today" As a result, the most dominating, and emotionally charged wordS, such as 'nag' and 'moan' impacted her subconscious mind the most, and this is what ended up happening. These emotionally charged words became the 'goal' for her subconscious to act upon. Whatever you speak about is what will dominate. It made no difference that she said she must not do that, because the words 'nag' and 'moan' have more emotional impact than small unimportant words such as 'must not'. As soon as the words such as 'nag' and 'moan' are spoken, they become dominating thoughts. Thus, they themselves become the goal.

As long as she kept saying that, she would be subconsciously thinking about moaning and nagging, and she would end up doing that. The most dominant thoughts then affect our actions, and our behaviour. The solution? Say what you want instead of what you don't want. This is the difference between stating something positively and stating it negatively, even though the two sentences might mean the same thing. For example she could have said "I love Mike and get on great with him" or "I am so happy that Mike is in my life. We are both good listeners and show each other mutual respect" or "Mike has many good qualities. I compliment him often, because I love him".

Any of these affirmations would have helped massively to stop her from moaning at Mike. Why? Because the positive words in these sentences would become the dominant thoughts and that is what she would be motivated to do. Negative and positive thoughts cannot occupy the mind at the same time. One or the other must dominate. If we speak positively, it flushes out the negative. If we speak negatively, it flushes out the positive. You cannot expect to perform well if you are speaking negative words. Always say what you want, never what you don't want.

FOCUS

If you like it or not, what you speak about becomes your focus. Talk about nagging and nagging becomes your focus. Talk about getting on well with someone, and getting on well with them becomes your focus. Talk about failure, and failure becomes your focus. Talk about winning, and winning becomes your focus. But here's the interesting part; what you focus on, is what you attract. Whatever you continually focus on, you will attract into your life, in actual physical reality. So if you want to win, keep failure out of your mind. Don't talk about it, don't think about it and don't focus on it. Focus only on winning. I'm not saying that you shouldn't have a 'plan B' in case something goes wrong; I'm just saying that it shouldn't be focused on, or thought about. And it should be put at the back of your mind. You could liken it to having an insurance policy. Everyone needs insurance, whether its car insurance, home insurance, life insurance or whatever. But that doesn't mean that you continually go around thinking about your house burning down, your car getting stolen or dying young. Although they are possibilities, we don't focus on them.

I remember hearing an American pilot talking about the importance of thinking the right thoughts during combat. He had flown carrier based aircraft during World War Two, against Japanese shipping. He said that "Although you were aware of the extreme dangers, and all the terrible things that could happen to you, these things had to be put at the back of your mind, otherwise you wouldn't be able to survive". If you put the worst possible things at the forefront of your mind, you will get the jitters and you will attract it. You need to keep failure out of your mind and visualise only what you want to happen.

Imagine driving a car, and as you drove along the road, instead of looking straight ahead, you continually focused on the kerb. What do you think would happen? Eventually you would crash! And it wouldn't be surprising if you did hit the kerb, because that's what you were focusing on. How can you expect to get safely to your destination if you were focusing on something else? You can't. What you focus on is what you move towards.

Many years ago, we had a school gymnasium, in which one of the physical education teachers had constructed an assault course. It consisted of all kinds of obstacles, such as climbing frames which went all the way up to the roof and metal bars and ropes for swinging on. One part of the assault course required us to leap from one part of the climbing frame and cling onto a horizontal metal bar, which was suspended about eight feet off the ground. If you caught hold of the bar, you were fine. But if not you landed on the mat below.

One particular person, who I will call Joe, had missed the bar, and even although he landed on the mat, he had twisted his arm. Everyone gasped because they felt sorry for him, but the injury turned out not to be serious. Fortunately, everyone else either caught the bar, or if they had fallen, fell safely onto the mat.

Anyway, the following week (as we had our physical education every Friday) we had the same assault course. Everyone was present including Joe. Then it came time to make the mid-air jump, from the climbing frame, to the metal bar. When it came time to make the jump, everyone watched as each person made the jump. There were cheers as each person successfully caught the bar in mid-flight. Then it was Joe's turn.

The hall went silent. I could almost feel what everyone else was feeling and I'm sure they were thinking the same thing as me. We were thinking about the fall Joe had the previous week but were hoping it wouldn't be a repeat performance. He suddenly leaped…. and fell again, hurting his arm. We couldn't believe it. Whether Joe could sense what we were thinking, I don't know. Maybe the pressure got to him. But it turned out that just before Joe jumped, he had a vivid picture in his mind of the fall he had, the previous week. He was so afraid of falling for a second time and hurting his arm, that he actually created a mental picture of it happening again. This then became the goal for his subconscious to achieve. Instead of visualising himself making a successful jump, he visualised failure. His subconscious then lined up all his actions with this goal in mind. As a result he fell.

VISUALISE A POSITIVE OUTCOME

Realise that we think in pictures, not in words. Although our subconscious is affected by words, it acts upon the mental images, or pictures we hold in our minds. Whatever we picture in our minds, most often will be looked upon as a goal to achieve. This might sound like a contradiction but it's not, because our words have the power to create the mental images in the first place. This principle, if you can grasp hold of what I am telling you, can work miracles in your life. Maybe you cannot get thoughts of failure out of your mind. Maybe you have a hard time visualising yourself being successful. Well, there is hope. You can use words to create a new mental picture of success. In the case of Joe missing the bar in gymnasium, I can fully sympathise with his fear. But at the same time, there are things Joe could have done to help himself. Prior to going into the gym, he could have visualised himself in his imagination successfully catching the bar. He could have actually done some role-playing in the privacy of his own home, by having an imitation bar, or something resembling a bar, and practiced successfully catching it. Remember the subconscious can't tell the difference between a real experience and one vividly imagined.

He could have used affirmations to flush out thoughts of failure. As he visualised himself catching the bar, he could have said things like "Great! I've done it!" or "Thank you God for helping me catch the bar". He could even have used a third person affirmation. This is an affirmation which 'you' speak, but you are pretending the voice is from someone else, such as someone giving you a compliment. In this case, he could have used a third person affirmation, pretending the teacher was giving him a compliment. He could have said "Well done Joe, I knew you could do it!" This often has a more powerful effect because sometimes we listen more to other people, than we do to ourselves.

These words would have created a vivid mental picture of him succeeding, along with the winning feeling and the positive emotions that go with it. Thus, he would be programming himself for success. The more often it gets done (or practiced), the more imbedded in the subconscious it gets. When practicing a successful outcome, this is exactly what you are trying to do. If you are faced with a difficult task, instead of telling yourself its difficult, tell yourself "It's easy" and it will become easier. Your mind will find ways to make it easier. Mentally you will look at it differently, and then it will become easier in reality. You might see ways to do it, that you would not normally have seen, because you were 'blinded to it'.

MENTAL GIANTS WIN

How do you view failure? Do you focus on the pain and the disappointment, or do you focus on the lesson it taught you? Average people focus on the former, but winners, although they hurt just as much, learn to focus on the lessons learned. I believe this is one of the main reasons people quit. The people who quit are so absorbed by the pain and disappointment that they can't see the lesson failure is trying to teach them. They may even be angry, and their anger is blinding them to the learning the lesson. Having been involved in network marketing I have also had to get used to failure and disappointment. There have been times when I came close to quitting through sheer disappointment and frustration, but I never actually did. As bad as the disappointment might have been, God always seem to cause something good to happen to keep me in, or He would get someone to counsel me and 'see the light'. I am so glad (now) that I did stay in!

There was a time when I had asked one of my close friends if he was interested in looking at the business idea, or coming along to one of our meetings. He said "No" he wasn't interested. A few weeks later, he showed up at one of the meetings in someone else's group. You can imagine what I thought! That was a bitter pill for me to swallow, and there was more to come! Other people who I was going to approach, I didn't approach quickly enough, and they were sponsored by other people. I regularly saw them at the meetings after that, which continually rubbed salt into the wounds. But I had to rise above it if I was going to survive. I had the feeling God was testing me. I saw people who got in, after me, pass me. But in spite of this, I had a choice. I could quit, or go on. That was within my control, and always would be. I decided to go on, in spite of the pain I felt inside. Something deep down inside of me kept telling me, "You need to go on! If you quit, then you 'will' be a failure. If you quit, what else is there? Keep going, you're not going to die!"

Often when we fail, it can be something on our part that needs a little fine-tuning. Average people don't like to hear that because they don't want to change, and they don't want to take responsibility. But winners accept they have shortcomings, are willing to learn, and are quite willing to change for the better. Winners are also teachable.

I remember when I first started learning to drive. (incidentally, this was a long time before joining network marketing) I had spent a lot of time and money getting lessons. After several months, my instructor said I was good enough to go in for my test. I went in for it and failed. My response to failure was negative. I was so disappointed and ticked off, that I didn't even bother to think about driving lessons for a whole year. I wasn't interested anymore. But that was a dumb response really!

What I should have done is get right back out there and persisted. Why waste time? Every time you take a break, you lose momentum. The problem with that attitude towards failure is that it becomes habit forming, and affects other areas of your life. If you take that attitude once, then you find it easy to quit the next time. You might quit when it comes to business, or you might quit keeping fit. You might quit your marriage instead of trying to sort things out. No-one has ever achieved greatly in life, by quitting when the going gets tough. And they never will. Instead, you need to form the habit of persistence in 'all' areas of your life. You need to forge ahead, no matter what you are up against. Make persistence the hallmark of your character. It will pay you handsomely in the future, and you will develop the character of a winner.

CHAPTER 5

BELIEVE IN YOURSELF

f you don't believe in yourself, who else is going to? If you want to improve your lifestyle and achieve your dreams, you need to believe in yourself. Everything you require, in order to be successful, you already possess. I'm not talking about money or anything externally; I'm talking about your physical and mental capacity. There is nothing someone else has, that you don't. The only thing that is stopping you from achieving your dreams is you. If you were to examine the chemical make-up of every human being, you would find that they are made up of exactly the same chemical elements; the exact same as you! We are all made up of atoms. We are all composed of protons, electrons and neutrons, and we all have the capacity to think what we want. If you don't believe that you are worthy of success, then that is exactly where the problem lies; your beliefs are false. You need to work on changing your beliefs. You have the ability, but if you don't believe you have the ability, then you will defeat yourself.

If you don't believe in yourself, at least there is hope. Your thoughts can be changed, and belief can be developed, by changing what goes into your mind. You need to believe in your abilities, and that you are capable of achieving whatever you want to achieve. If you don't feel very confident just now, or you are not too sure of your abilities, then you need to believe you can improve. That, you must believe. Reading books will help you to do that. You need to believe that you have the potential to become better, and that God put the potential inside of you, to be much better. The only difference between successful people and average people is that they think differently. You will find that all high achievers believe in themselves. They usually have more self confidence, they think bigger, instead of thinking small, and they take action. They don't just talk about things, or wish things would happen, they 'make them happen' by taking action.

I'll be completely honest with you. A few years ago, maybe about five years prior to this writing, I didn't think I could write a book. At that point I had read stacks of positive thinking books, maybe a couple of hundred, over the space of a few years. Yet I still didn't think I had what it takes to write a book. The thought of writing a book had crossed my mind, but I thought I wasn't intelligent enough, and that everyone who wrote these books were geniuses. So I dismissed the thought and forgot about it. In other words, I didn't believe in myself enough. So, what actually stopped me? The answer is ME! I stopped myself, by my own negative thinking. 'Thought' is very powerful; it can cause success or failure, happiness or unhappiness. But we decide our thoughts. When I 'thought' I couldn't write a book, the key word in that sentence is 'thought'. That's all it was-- just a thought, not a fact. You might be thinking, "So what changed, that caused you to write a book?" Well, not too long ago, a female associate of mine told me that her husband had got his first book published. I was so impressed and inspired, that it ignited a spark within me. I had never met an author in my life before, until now. It was then that I decided to give it a shot. But there's more to it than that. I felt (and still do feel) that I have a very important message to share with people. It was this burning desire to share with people what I had learned, that made me want to write.

You do not have to be a genius to write a book. Anyone can write about what they have experienced and what they have learned. You can do it too, if you have the desire. Remember what Henry Ford said, "You can if you think you can, but if you think you can't, you're right too!"

At first, the thought of writing a book might seem overwhelming. Thinking of writing a book may seem daunting to some people. But what you do is you break it down into small achievable chunks. The first thing I did was decide on a title for the book (what the book will be about). Secondly, I decided what each chapter will be about (a name for each chapter). Then I broke each chapter down into subheadings, and concentrated on that. A page at a time, a subheading at a time, I wrote the book. As a result of focusing only on the task at hand (writing a page at a time) the book wrote itself. Yet, if I had listened to my earlier belief, I would never have taken that step, and you would not be reading this book just now. It's the same with setting goals. You might have a goal to make a certain amount of money every week, but if you break it down into daily goals, and concentrate on making a certain amount every day, the weekly goal will take care of itself. It's not so much the circumstances, but how you look at the circumstances that matters. It's amazing how powerful beliefs are, and how they shape our lives, either for the better or worse, depending on what is believed. False beliefs limit and restrict us, while the truth sets us free, and opens up opportunities. The problem is not that we don't have what it takes; the problem is 'believing' we don't have what it takes. There's a big difference. There may be some things at this very moment which are holding you back, which are false, but you are convinced are true. Yet, if you believe them, they will be true for you, and continue to have power over you. Therefore, you need to smash these false beliefs, once and for all. Why not use some affirmations such as:

I AM VALUABLE
I BELIEVE IN MYSELF
I HAVE NO LIMITS
GOD GAVE ME AS MUCH POTENTIAL AS ANYONE ELSE
EVERY DAY IS A NEW BEGINNING
I WAS BORN TO WIN
I'VE GOT EVERYTHING IT TAKES TO SUCCEED
I AM CONFIDENT AND COURAGEOUS

Once I had written my first book, there was a bit of an anti-climax. I got such a buzz out of writing it, that when I was finished, I was left wondering what I would do next. I still didn't have a publisher at that stage, so I was going to be busy trying to find one, but I also wanted to keep writing. I was operating on blind faith that I would get it published, yet some people (some who were quite close to me) kept reminding me that all my work might be in vain, and that I might not get a publisher. I had to mentally shut these comments out of my mind and remind myself that I wasn't going to give up until I did find a publisher. I didn't care if I died of old age in the process; I wasn't going to give up no matter how many rejections I got. I had many rejections from publishers, before I eventually got an offer of a contract. During this time of rejection, I had some dangerous thoughts. I began to doubt my work. I began to wonder if the reason I was getting rejected was because my work wasn't good enough. I began to picture myself at 100 years old, sitting writing letters to publishers, still trying to get my book published. I pictured people ridiculing me, saying "Still not got a publisher yet?" Then I began to have an inner dialogue with myself, which went something like this; "Maybe you're out of your league. Maybe you think you're a big shot, but you're not really. You'll be the author who only writes one book in his entire life. Maybe writing isn't for you after all?"

Then suddenly I snapped out of it and thought "What the hell are you doing thinking stupid thoughts like that? You've just written a positive book! Don't you think you should take some of your own advice? Have faith! Keep trying! Remember, God responds to faith, not doubt!" I realised the damage I was doing to myself and vowed not to think like that again. I also realised these thoughts were from the devil, and they weren't good. Remember that whenever you try to do some kind of work for God, the devil will do everything he can to try and stop you. He'll plant the seeds of doubt and discouragement in your mind, to stop you being effective for God.

But then I was faced with another dilemma. I wanted to keep writing, but didn't think I knew enough to write another book. I thought (notice the word 'thought') that I had written all I could write about. The emotional pain was great. I thought that I had just found a new avenue; writing, and I loved doing it, but now I wasn't able to do what I loved doing because I had written everything I thought I could write about. Then out of the blue, someone gave me an idea for a title. I was overjoyed because I suddenly realised there was a multitude of things to write about.

But I also realised something else; WE ARE ONLY LIMITED BY OUR OWN IMAGINATION. Walt Disney said, "If you can dream it, you can do it." The only thing stopping you is you!

If you find yourself thinking self defeating thoughts, you need to stop immediately and tell yourself the opposite. Always tell yourself what you want to be true, or you will limit yourself, and set yourself up for failure.

When I was thinking I didn't know enough to write another book, I could have used affirmations such as :

- "I GET NEW IDEAS FOR WRITING BOOKS EVERY DAY"

- "WRITING COMES EASY TO ME, AND SO DO IDEAS"

- "MY IDEAS FOR BOOKS ARE UNLIMITED"

- "ITS GOOD FUN THINKING OF A NEW TITLE, BECAUSE THERE ARE SO MANY TO CHOOSE FROM"

By using such techniques, you are programming your mind to go 180 degrees in the opposite direction (which is what you want). Your subconscious will now be working in your favour, instead of against you. Oliver Wendell Holmes said "Once a man's mind is stretched by a new idea, it never goes back to its original dimension". When you do something you didn't believe you could do, new patterns are formed deep in your subconscious, and you 'grow' mentally. Your self image changes, (who you believe you are). The amazing thing is, the more you do it, the more you believe you are able to do it.

You will be a different person, as a result of reading this book because new patterns will have been formed in your subconscious mind. New beliefs may have been formed and self imposed limitations may have been destroyed. Therefore, in that respect, you are a different person.

BE A POSSIBILITY THINKER

Forget about whether you feel something is true or not, that has nothing to do with it. Just tell yourself what you want to be true, and keep repeating it. Even Hitler recognised the power in this principle; that if a 'lie' is repeated often enough, eventually it will be believed. The mind will accept 'anything' if it is told often enough.

If you can't see a way, tell yourself "There is a way" Your mind will look for ways, no matter how 'impossible' it might seem. And as long as you are telling yourself that, your mind will never stop looking, and it won't give up. But the minute you say "I can't do it" or "There is no way", you have just slammed the door shut on any possibilities of finding a way. As soon as you tell yourself you are defeated, then you are. Or if you tell yourself "It's impossible", then it is. Your subconscious accepts what you have said (or thought) and you are defeated.

In 1942 the British 'Desert Rats' were engaged in a long bloody conflict with Erwin Rommel's, forces in North Africa. For a long time, it was stalemate. The Germans would over-run the British, and then the British would over-run the Germans. The port of Benghazi changed hands five times. The Germans had superiority in weapons and equipment. The German anti-tank guns could hit the British tanks before the British could even get within striking distance. But it was when defeat stared the British in the face, that things swung dramatically their way. Through sheer courage and persistence, the tables began to turn. This often happens, not just in war, but in life. If we persist, no matter what the odds are, or how tough it is, things have an uncanny way of working out, often in our favour. Eventually the British did defeat Rommel, but they had to believe it was possible, even when things looked impossible.

This is often what separates winners from losers. A person who can't see a way, quits because it looks impossible. But a person who wins at the game of life, persists because they believe the way will present itself, as time goes on. One person has faith, the other does not. Anyone can believe in what is seen. It takes a person with faith to believe in what is unseen. You also need to have faith in your abilities, and your ability to become better. If you don't have faith in your abilities just now, then you must believe that you can develop the abilities. Why not use affirmations to help you develop belief in yourself?

The good thing about affirmations is that you can have them tailor-made to suit your own unique situation. The affirmations I have used in this chapter are just examples. You might want to affirm something different, depending on your own unique situation. If for example, you talk too much, then you might want to affirm "I am a good listener" Or if you have a short temper, you might want to affirm "I am cool, calm and collective at all times". But you must decide for yourself, depending on what you want to achieve.

If you were at a business seminar and the speaker suddenly announced that only 5 percent of the people who got involved in the business, ever became extremely wealthy, and that other 95 percent only made modest amounts of money. What would you tell yourself? Would you think "Darn! I knew he was going to say that! I guess I'll never be rich" or would you tell yourself "I know 5 percent is a small amount, but I'm going to do whatever it takes to make sure I'm in the 5 percent group. I'm going to find out what they do differently, that the other 95 percent don't, and I'm going to emulate them. I'm a five-percenter".

What you tell yourself will determine where you end up. It's as simple as that. It's all to do with how you talk to yourself. How you talk to yourself will determine your actions. Your actions then determine where you end up. Your inner voice will always determine where you end up, unless you change it and start telling yourself different things. Why tell yourself something that will cause you to fail?

The other thing to ask yourself is "Why do you believe the way you do?" If you said to yourself "I'll bet I'll end up in the 95 percent group" Why do you believe that? It could be due to a lack of confidence, or because you've never had much previous success in your life. But more often than not, it's because of past experiences. People have a hard time believing things can be better, because they've been so used to mediocrity in the past. Their track record up until now hasn't been anything startling, so why should the future be anything different? Well, this is a loser's way of thinking, and you need to SNAP OUT OF IT RIGHT NOW! This is a big mistake which is common to many people. They allow their past to control their future. But your past will only control your future if you let it! Your life can be different from this moment onwards, if you decide to make it different. If you keep telling yourself you're in the 95 percent group, then you always will be! But if you decide today is going to be a new beginning, you can create that too, but only if you are willing to make some changes. You cannot expect to get into the 5 percent group by telling yourself you're in the 95 percent group. Your words have to change, if you want the results to change

If you were writing a book and it was going to cost you money to get it published, and the publisher said to you "I'll be honest with you, the vast majority of people fail to make it big. Only a very small percentage ever become bestsellers" Would it put you off going ahead with it? If it did, then it is because you are talking negatively to yourself. But if you believe in yourself and your work, you would talk positively to yourself. You would expect your book to do well, and not only re-coup your expenditure, but also to make a handsome profit. You would expect people to be interested in it. You would visualise it being read by millions of people. Therefore, you would be far more likely to take a calculated risk. This seemingly small difference in self-talk has huge long term ramifications (some might say consequences) A different inner voice produces a different course of action, which produces different results.

DON'T BE INTIMIDATED

Sometimes we talk negatively to ourselves because we are comparing ourselves to other people. We might find ourselves in a situation where we are learning something new, such as learning to drive a car, or learning how to perform a particular task, and we feel out of our depth. We might look at how well other people are doing it and get discouraged. But to compare yourself to other people is pointless, because you are not in competition with anyone but yourself. These other people were at some stage, at the same level you are at now, because they also had to learn. The only difference is that they have had more practice than you.

If you begin to feel discouraged, it is at that very point that you need to take control. You can't afford to talk negatively to yourself or you will set yourself up for failure. No matter how good the other person is, remind yourself that at one point, they were a beginner, just like you. Also, tell yourself that no matter how good they are just now, you have the capability to become just as good as them, maybe even better! Don't limit yourself with negative self-talk, tell yourself what you want to be true, and your subconscious will respond.

I remember when I was first learning how to drive. It all seemed so complicated. There was so much to remember, so many things to do, all at the same time, that I thought I'd never be able to drive. (But that's all it was-- just a thought, not a fact) Then one of my friends or relatives would jump in the car, and what I had been struggling to do, they done in an instant, and off they went. They made it look so easy. The difference was that they had been doing this for several years; I had only been doing it for a few weeks. Now that I've been driving for many years, what once seemed so complicated to me, I now find so easy. In fact, so easy that I don't really have to think about it, because it is all done subconsciously.

The danger is that if you are having a hard time learning something and you start comparing yourself to other people; it can cause you to put yourself down (telling yourself lies instead of the truth) which leads to discouragement. You end up placing yourself psychologically away below them, which makes you feel worse. Instead, you need to be projecting yourself (mentally) upwards, into where they are now. You need to visualise yourself doing what they are doing now, and doing it just as well. Get out of the two-tier mentality of superior and inferior. Instead realise you are both equal, the only difference is that they have had more practice than you. See yourself with the same capabilities, because you have. The only difference is, yours need to be nurtured and developed.

Personally, I don't look down on anyone, but I don't look up either. Why should I look up to anyone if they have the same capabilities as me? Why should I look down on anyone if they have the same capabilities as me? There is only one Person I look up to, and that is Almighty God. Sure, there are many people I like and admire, but in terms of value, they are just another human being, neither superior nor inferior. They have desires and fears just like I do, because we are all human. Their accomplishments may be superior, but they are not a superior person.

If you start telling yourself other people are superior, or have some superior qualities that you don't, it will be similar to putting a noose around your neck. Only it won't be a physical noose, it will be a psychological noose, which will limit and restrict you. Once accepted, you will then 'live-out' these beliefs as though they were true. Even if they are based on falsehood, they will be true for you, because your subconscious will create them. Our physical lives are always a manifestation of our inner voice, and always will be.

If you are learning how to drive, why not tell yourself "I'm improving every day" or "I can do anything I put my mind to" You could even affirm "I'm so happy I've now passed my driving test! It feels great!" and put as much emotion into it as possible. Remember that your subconscious responds to emotion. Why not buy a card which says "Congratulations, You've passed!" and put it somewhere you can see it every day. Now some people might scoff at this and say that you're setting yourself up for even greater disappointment if you fail. Negative thinking!! The fact that they've said that means they are already thinking about failure. But actually the opposite is true. Your subconscious is more likely to line up your actions with the 'goal' which is set for it, which is passing your test. Remember that affirmations are based on the premise that you are mentally creating something which doesn't yet exist. You don't wait until it exists before you say it, because it might never happen. Goal setting and affirmations are about speaking something into existence which you want to exist. The goal or 'target' must come first, not after, because your subconscious won't have anything to aim at.

If you were trying to learn about computers, don't tell yourself that you don't have a clue about computers, because you don't want that. Instead tell yourself things like: "I love working with computers. They are really straight-forward and very interesting" or "I am learning new things every day about computers. It's easy and its good fun!"

Many years ago I found myself being a spectator at a martial arts class. There were some new people in the class, but most of them had been there for a long time and were well experienced. I remember the instructor saying to the new people at the interval "Don't be intimidated or discouraged because some of these other guys are better than you. Many times I've seen some of the new people improve to such a level that they've actually passed some of the well experienced ones". He was trying to convey to them that how good you are just now, is not your limit. You are far from your potential, so don't limit yourself by believing that you are as good as you can get. None of us will ever reach our full potential, because there's always room for improvement. You have within you, at this precise moment, everything you need to become great. You just need to believe it.

EVERY DAY IS A NEW BEGINNING

We must be careful not to let a negative past distort our inner voice and affect our future. Often when we have a negative experience, and we are faced with the same situation again, we remind ourselves of past failures and end up talking negatively to ourselves. By doing that, we can actually end up creating the very thing we want to avoid. We must learn from failure, but mentally flush it, as soon as we have learned the lesson. After that, it should not be thought of again. From then on we should only be focusing on the task at hand, and focusing on what we want to happen. In other words, become future orientated, instead of past orientated.

I found this quite a challenge, especially when I became involved in network marketing. When I was showing the presentation regularly, I got all kinds of reactions from people. Some were polite, some were rude, some were interested and some were not. Some were time-wasters and pretended they were interested but didn't want to say no. Others made it absolutely clear that they wanted nothing to do with it. On one occasion I was actually told to get out of a couples house. I had only started to explain about five minutes of the presentation and they accused me of all kinds of things and thought I was trying to manipulate them. They told me on no uncertain terms, to get out and don't come back. Sometimes things like that can shake you, especially if you're new in the business and inexperienced like I was. Often things like that can cause people to quit. People who do quit, will never get very far in life because that's not how the battle is won. Only through sheer persistence and facing your fears will you achieve your dreams. But the point I want to make is this ; I had another appointment booked with a different couple two nights later. When I went along to show them the presentation, this negative experience was very vivid in my mind, to the point that I was actually expecting this couple to blow their top and throw me out of their house as well. Isn't it strange how we expect our future to be like our past?

I was very surprised when they were polite and respectful. I thought to myself "What's wrong? They're being polite!" I think God was trying to show me that the vast majority of people are good. As I became more experienced in the business and read more books, I learned not take with you, negative experiences from the past. As soon as I walked into their room, It didn't matter what else was going on in my life, or what had happened at the last presentation, all that got put to the back of my mind. If I wanted to think about any of that stuff, I would wait until the presentation was over and I was away from their house. I had to realise that every day is a new beginning and that every person and every situation is unique. I had to focus only on the present moment, while visualising a positive outcome. I had to expect them to be friendly and expect them to be interested because this would come across in my body language and my attitude. My subconscious would then begin to line up all my actions with the end goal in mind. The 'end-goal' being whatever I pictured happening, whether success or failure. Either way, I would attract it.

Sometimes I would have two presentations booked in the same evening, maybe two hours apart. I might have just been verbally 'chewed out' at the first presentation, but I could not take any of this with me into the next presentation, or it would mess me up and affect my attitude. I had to flush it, and go in with a new attitude, and tell myself that they're going to be interested, regardless of what had just happened.

If you want to succeed at anything in life, you need to become mentally tough. You need to be able to handle rejection and ridicule, as well as visualising a positive outcome and maintaining a positive attitude. The best way to do this is with the help of a personal development programme, which was discussed in the previous chapter. The human mind is not strong enough on its own, to stand up to all the negativity, unless you are counteracting it with something positive. Only by controlling what you say, what you read and what you listen to, can you withstand and overcome all the negativity. Only then can you achieve your dreams.

I often compare the human mind to a football. When the ball is pumped up properly it can be used to its maximum potential. It can be kicked about, up and down a field for 90 minutes and it is still in good condition. In other words, it can stand up to it. But it is only because of what is inside (the air pressure), that it can take the forces from the outside. If it wasn't pumped up on the inside, it would be absolutely useless. It wouldn't be able to take a beating and still be able to bounce high in the air. So it is with your mind, only instead of being pumped up with air, you need to pump it up with positive thoughts. Then, not only will you be able to stand up to all the negativity, but you will also be able to achieve your dreams.

YOU DON'T NEED THE APPROVAL OF OTHER PEOPLE

In life, you are going to be criticised no matter what you do, so you might as well get used to that now. If you're going to get criticised, it's better to be criticised for pursuing your dreams, rather than be criticised for doing nothing. If you're going to get criticised, you might as well be criticised for doing what's right, rather than what's wrong. If you are doing what's right in the eyes of God, and you believe in what you're doing, don't worry about criticism. You might as well accept the fact that it's impossible to please everyone, and some people might not approve of what you are doing. But that's their problem, not yours.

When Jesus was here on earth, He offended many people with his teaching. But did that stop Him? No, and neither should it have, because He was here to do the will of his Father, not to please men. He was here to tell them what they needed to hear, not necessarily what they wanted to hear.

Jesus said to the Pharisees, "And why do you break the command of God for the sake of your tradition?" (Mat 15: 3)

"Thus you nullify the word of God for the sake of your tradition. You hypocrites! Isaiah was right when he prophesied about you:

"These people honour me with their lips, but their hearts are far from me. They worship me in vain; their teachings are but rules taught by men" (Mat 15: 6--8)

Later, in the book of Matthew, Jesus says "Woe to you, teachers of the law and Pharisees, you hypocrites! You travel over land and sea to win a single convert, and when he becomes one, you make him twice as much a son of hell as you are." (Mat 23: 15)

You need to accept criticism, rather than fight it. By doing this, you will actually make things easier on yourself. Rather than let criticism annoy you, learn to laugh it off. You might even get to the stage where you actually feel sorry for the people who criticise you, because they can't see what you can see, and consequently don't have the opportunity you have. When you have committed to do something which you believe is right, you need to stand by your guns, regardless of how much criticism you get. Politicians are adept at this, to the extent that some of them are downright arrogant. But that is going to the extreme because there is no excuse for arrogance. But you do need to stand by your convictions, while maintaining a positive attitude.

The sad reality is that not everyone is going to support you and your idea. Some people may be jealous of you, and some will want you to fail, because your success will make them look bad. Even sadder, is the fact that often it's the people closest to us that can hurt us the most. I remember one woman in particular who had a business opportunity. She quickly caved in to criticism from her husband, and she couldn't handle the fact that she thought she had offended her friends. Her husband was a control-freak and didn't want her to become financially independent, because he would have felt threatened. He thought that if she made enough money that she might not need him anymore. Actually his real problem was fear. So he started ridiculing her and calling her all kinds of names. He would often say "So you're going to be a great big business woman are you?" But the crazy thing is this ; how can anyone expect a relationship or marriage to work, if two people are pulling in different directions? It's a recipe for disaster! For any relationship to work, both people need to be pulling in the same direction, not opposite directions. Both need to be supportive of each other, and both need to be on the 'same team'. There needs to be love instead of competition. Your partner is 'not' your competitor. They are your partner!

Anyway she eventually quit because of the criticism from her husband and also due to the fact that when she invited her friends around to see the presentation, they were deeply offended that it wasn't a party with food and wine. She couldn't handle the fact that they were offended, even although she had told them before-hand that it was strictly a business presentation. I must admit that I felt genuinely sorry for her, not only because of the ridicule from her husband, but because deep down she didn't believe in herself enough to make a stand.

I am not a marriage counsellor, or any kind of relationship expert, so I won't even try to give advice concerning that side of things. But the point I want to make is this, you cannot be wishy washy and expect to succeed. You cannot be emotionally weak, if you want great success. You cannot be weak-minded or afraid of criticism, instead, you need to get used to it.

On a positive note, I've heard of couples in the same business who disagreed with each other, as to whether they should get involved or not. In one case, the wife didn't want to do it but her husband did. Not only did she not want to do it, but she didn't want him to do it either. To which he turned round and said "Honey, things are going to be better round here, if you like it or not!" That's what I call making a stand! That's what I call believing in yourself!

Eventually she accepted the fact that he was going to do it, and she gradually began to support him, especially when she saw the effort he was putting in. After a while, she joined him in the business, and eventually they both became extremely successful. Their marriage also improved in the process. Today, their marriage is stronger than ever, probably due in large part to the amount of books they've read, and also due to the fact that they are pulling in the same direction.

One sure way to make yourself miserable is trying to live your life pleasing everybody. Don't get me wrong, I'm not saying we shouldn't care or help people, but we should never get to a point where every decision we make, is based on what everybody else might think. But some people are so afraid of criticism that they live their lives that way. This is absolutely futile, because it is impossible to please everybody. For example, in the world of politics, it doesn't matter how popular a prime minister or president is, there is always an opposing party. Which shows that even although millions might agree with them, there is always some that don't. But do politicians change their policies just because some people don't agree with them? Of course not! I'm not saying whether a particular policy is good or bad, I'm just saying that if a politician changed his or her policies every time someone criticised them, they wouldn't get very far.

Jesus was perfect. He performed miracles, healed the sick and raised people from the dead and did nothing but good. But look what happened to Him! He was perfect, and they crucified him! So if that happened to our Lord, I think we can expect some criticism now and again.

In war, many decisions have to be made which are later considered controversial, such as the firebombing of Dresden and the dropping of the atomic bombs on Japan. It often amazes me how some of these armchair critics fail to recognise the heroism and bravery of our armed forces. Of course there would be critics. Even today, there are critics. But someone had to make the decision, regardless of criticism. In war, it's them or us, and it's that simple. You don't win wars by feeling sorry for your enemy. In my opinion, the critics don't see the big picture, they focus only on one aspect of things; the horror. They don't look at the fact that in both cases it helped to shorten the war. They forget that it's easy to criticise when the war is won and it's all over, but at the actual time, no-one knew if we would win or not. They forget about the number of Allied casualties, and that the bombing of Dresden in early 1945, helped make way for the Russians coming in from the east. They forget that the Japanese preferred death to surrender, and were eager to die for their emperor. Many of the Japanese suicide pilots actually signed their names in their own blood, in order to increase their chances of selection.

If the Americans hadn't dropped the atomic bombs, it would have meant invading the Japanese mainland itself. This would have meant the war lasting much longer, and a far greater amount of lives would have been lost, than was lost in the dropping of the two atomic bombs put together. If we had listened to the critics, a far greater amount of lives would have been lost, both Japanese and American.

But the point I want to make is this; there would have been criticism either way, whether the bombs had been dropped or not. If the bombs hadn't been dropped, people could have accused the president of allowing the war to go on much longer, un-necessarily. They could have accused him of causing further un-necessary loss of lives, because he had the power to use these weapons, but decided not to use them. Therefore, a decision had to be made, regardless of what critics thought, or what they would think in the future.

One veteran who survived the war, summed it up this way ; "They gave their today, for our tomorrow" The last thing we should be doing is criticising them. We should be thankful for our freedom and remember the price that was paid for it. If you try and please everybody, that's when you usually make the worst decisions, because you are making them for the wrong reasons.

The solution? Do what you believe is right, regardless of what people think.

DEVELOPING YOUR SUIT OF ARMOUR

Sometimes the criticism we receive is more severe, and is directed at us personally, rather than what we are doing. People might say things like "He'll never make it. He's no good at that" or "What makes you think you could do something like that? You can't do that!" This is when it becomes crucial to develop your suit of armour, psychologically speaking. If not, then your chances of persisting are greatly reduced. People who fail to develop their suit of armour, usually end up quitting. Most people I saw, who quit the network marketing business, were people who never done much. They failed to share the presentation with people and they failed to develop their suit of armour by reading books and going to seminars.

They would make comments such as "I don't like reading" or "I can't afford to go to the seminar". These are not the words of a winner. No-one will take constant negative bombardment for long, unless it is counteracted by something positive. Instead, a winner says "I'm going to read, and I'm going to do whatever it takes" They also say "Regardless of my financial situation, I'm going to find the money for the seminar, even if it means cutting back on something else".

It's seemingly small differences like these that mean the difference between success and failure. One person develops their suit of armour and succeeds, while the other person fails to develop it and fails. All the 'little differences' put together, make a huge difference, long term. With your suit of armour, you eventually get to a point that you are so used to criticism that it doesn't even bother you. But that can only happen by enduring it, not by avoiding it.

Sadly, when some people are criticised, they begin to doubt themselves and wonder if their critics could be right. The key word there is 'doubt'. Remember, doubt is a negative emotion and is the opposite of belief. You should never make your decisions based on negative emotions. Neither can you have faith if you have doubt, because they are opposites. Instead, have faith in yourself, and your ability to improve. Have faith that God is helping you, because He is. If you have faith, then you cannot have doubt, because the two cannot co-exist.

So how do develop your suit of armour when people are criticising you? You do it by counteracting the criticism with something positive. For example, if someone tells you, you don't have what it takes, don't get angry or sit around getting depressed, instead combat it by reading from a positive book. That way, you are responding positively. It's a bit like playing a sport such as fencing or boxing. Every time your opponent makes a dig at you, you don't just take it, you make a counter-move. But whatever you do, don't dwell on the criticism and let it dominate your thinking. If it is dominating your thinking, reading from a positive book will help to flush it out and will help you to develop belief in yourself. Never respond to adversity with negative emotions, or things will get worse and you will feel worse. Always respond positively.

You might talk to someone who steals your dream, and tells you that everyone else who tried your idea ended up broke and disillusioned. In that case, you could get in touch with one of your colleagues in the business (often referred to as a mentor) who meets two main requirements. Firstly, they must have your interest at heart, and secondly they must be more successful than you. Alternatively, you could listen to a motivational CD. It is only by making positive responses like these, that you are going to succeed. And it is only by habitually responding in this way, that you will start to develop belief in yourself. People who respond negatively don't last long in any endeavour. Neither do they develop belief in themselves.

There have been times in the business when I've come home disappointed and depressed because things didn't turn out the way I thought they would. Someone who was interested, changed their mind, or didn't turn up. Sometimes their 'friends' talked them out of it. One particular night, I was suffering from severe disappointment, because a guy, who was a good friend of mine, seemed like he was very interested in the business, changed his mind and decided not to do it. I began to think success wasn't for me, and felt like I would never succeed.

I came home and decided to listen to a tape, in the hope that it might make me feel better. I was home alone. It was just me, the four walls and the tape. You know the feeling? I thought, "If this tape doesn't do it, I'm quitting!" I then listened to a guy who was financially independent, talk about an experience that was far worse than mine. It made my disappointment seem small, in comparison to his. It made me realise that I was still on the road to success and that disappointment is part of success. It also made me realise that part of developing belief in yourself, is going through the struggles. I'm sorry folks, if you don't want to hear that, but there's no other way! So I went to bed positive, instead of negative. I went to bed with hope, instead of depression. But the good news is that the more pain you endure, the more you will develop belief in yourself. From what I've observed, the people who endure the most believe in themselves the most.

I owe an enormous amount to the CD's and tapes. There have been many times that I'm sure I would have quit, if it hadn't been for a CD or tape. These tools played a vital role in keeping me in, and also developing self belief. If I had quit, instead of listening to a tape that night, you wouldn't be reading this book just now. All I can say is that it's worth it!! It's worth it, no matter what you have to go through!!

If you make a habit of developing your suit of armour, by controlling what goes into your mind, eventually you become (as one motivational speaker put it) 'Six feet four and bullet-proof'. That was a saying we had in the business, when you developed the ability to let criticism and negative comments just bounce off you. It was almost as if you had had so much of it, that you became immune to it. You can actually turn criticism to your advantage, and do it just to spite your critics. You can use your critics as motivation to succeed, and develop the "I'll show them!" mentality. I must admit, I've often done it, and still do!

REACHING YOUR GOALS

If you want to reach your goals and achieve your dreams, you need to believe that God wouldn't put a dream in your heart without giving you the necessary abilities to achieve it. Just the fact that you have a dream in your heart means that God believes in you; otherwise He wouldn't have given you the dream. But don't just look at your present surroundings and level of confidence, look ahead. Realise that you are changing all the time, and that even if you feel you don't have what it takes just now, that's okay, because it can be developed. God knows you've got problems; God knows I've got problems. He knows we've all got problems, so don't worry about it. Just make a start and step out on faith. Have faith that through persistent effort, you will develop whatever is required, to achieve your dreams.

God wants to help you solve your problems and He wants to help you overcome whatever is holding you back. He wants you to have a good self image so that you can be extremely successful. He knows that you cannot be effective for Him, without self confidence. Therefore God will help you to become confident. But the devil, also knowing this, will try and destroy your self confidence, so that you cannot be effective for God. The devil is like the negative inner voice that is always causing you to put yourself down and doubt yourself. The devil wants you to think that success is only meant for other people, and that you had better just settle for a life of mediocrity. It's the devil who whispers to you "Why are you doing this? Are you crazy? Why put yourself through all this pain? In short, the devil wants you to quit. The devil also wants to keep you broke and to have a poor self image. But what does the Bible have to say about overcoming? It says "Blessed is the man who perseveres under trial because when he has stood the test, he will receive the crown of life that God has promised to those who love Him" (James 1:12)

Just because you don't believe you have the abilities to achieve your dreams, doesn't mean the abilities aren't there, it just means you don't believe it. In other words, you believe a lie, instead of the truth. In a similar way, if you don't believe in gravity, does it mean gravity isn't there? Of course not. It just means you believe a lie. If you don't believe $2 + 2 = 4$, does that mean $2 + 2$ no longer equals 4? Of course not. $2 + 2$ will always equal 4. Even if the whole world refused to believe that $2 + 2 = 4$, it is still the truth, regardless of whether it is believed or not. In the same way, you have the capabilities to reach your goals and achieve your dreams, regardless if you believe it or not. It's a case of changing your beliefs. When you believe you have the ability, then you will believe the truth.

If you want to reach your goals, they need to be written down on paper, and they need to be somewhere you can see them every day, so that they can be absorbed by your mighty subconscious. People who say that they don't need to write their goals down because they 'know what their goals are' don't have the assistance of their mighty subconscious, because they are trying to do it through sheer conscious effort. They limit the resources of their minds to conscious thinking only, making it harder for themselves. Why exclude such a mighty powerhouse such as the subconscious, when it is just as easy to use it. It is similar to going to the ocean to collect water, having a bucket with you, not using it, and using a teaspoon instead. Why do that when you have a bucket?

When you write something down, you write on the mind. Remember, your subconscious is affected by everything which reaches it through the five senses. When you read, it goes in through your eyes, and affects your subconscious. When you use affirmations, it goes in through your ears and affects your subconscious. But if you don't write your goals down, it doesn't involve any of your senses, and doesn't impact your subconscious. Your goals are then limited to conscious thinking only, are far less effective, and are far more likely to be forgotten. Why limit and restrict yourself like that, when you have the power of the subconscious within you?

GOALS ARE IN CONCRETE, PLANS ARE IN SAND

If you set a goal and fail to achieve it, it doesn't mean that you abandon the goal. Neither does it mean you are a failure. You simply reset the goal and go after it again. And you keep going after it until you do achieve it. Instead of saying "I'll give it a try" you need to develop the attitude of "I will until". Some people get so disheartened when they fail, that they give up completely. But that's not what winners do, and that's not how they think. The goal should remain constant, but the plans to get there should be flexible. The strategy or approach may change many times in the pursuit of a goal, especially when it is discovered that a particular plan or strategy isn't working. The time frame for achieving it also needs to be flexible, but the end goal should be the same.

For example, a while back, I had a goal to rent out a property, which was in a good area, and would have made a handsome profit. Rental income had always appealed to me, and I had had this goal for quite some time. But due to certain circumstances and a certain course of events beyond my control, I was forced to sell it. Logically I didn't want to sell it, but financially I had no option. It was a bitter pill to swallow. I thought to myself "Just when it looks as though I'm getting ahead, I get knocked down" (negative self talk)

People started coming round to view it, and one potential buyer unknowingly rubbed salt into the wounds by saying "A lot of dealers buy these houses to rent out because they're very profitable" Psychologically, it felt as though someone was sticking a knife in me, because the words cut deep. I remember thinking to myself "Then why the hell are you selling it?" I had no choice. But here's the point; Just because I'd been defeated on this particular occasion, didn't mean I gave up on the goal of renting property. I didn't say "Well, I guess renting just isn't for me!" My goal to rent property remained the same. It just meant that I wasn't going to rent this particular property. My plans were in sand once again! But that's okay! Your plans can change as many times as you want, as long as the goal remains constant.

Because of the profit I made when I sold the house, I was able to buy two more houses, and I ended up in an even better position.

I still ended up renting out property; it's just that it was a different property. Never give up on the goal, no matter what happens! It doesn't mean it won't happen, it just means it might happen in a different way, and at a different time. Keep defeat out of your mind. Don't even think about it. Even if the odds are stacked massively against you and defeat looks inevitable, think success. Because this is what will be the goal for your subconscious. As long as the thought of winning is held in the conscious mind, winning will be the goal for the subconscious mind.

Before Thomas Edison invented the electric light bulb, he had failed thousands of times. It took him ten thousand attempts to succeed. But at no point did he give up on his goal. Each time he failed, he simply tried a different approach, until he did succeed. When asked if he felt like a failure because he had failed so many times, he replied "I have not failed; I have merely found ten thousand ways which didn't work". Only if he had given up completely, would he have failed. Although his plans were subject to change, his goal to invent the electric bulb remained constant. But how many people in a similar position might have given up and changed the goal, itself? Instead of persevering to invent the electric bulb, they might have said "To hell with this. I don't think I'm ever going to invent this bulb, I'm trying something else!" Sadly, that is what many people do every day in life. If they don't succeed when they think they should, or it doesn't happen quickly enough, they quit and try something else.

Is it any surprise that some people don't believe in themselves, or have a poor self image? Not really, because they have developed failure habits instead of success habits. They have developed the habit of quitting, instead of persevering. Apart from that, if your kids see you quitting at the slightest obstacle, what example are you giving them? You're teaching them by your actions, that when the going gets tough, you bail out. Children will learn more by your actions than by what you say. Remember, self confidence is gained or lost, depending on your response to events and situations. By changing your actions and facing your fears, you will change who believe you are. You will develop self confidence and improve your self-image.

Some people have their goals in sand and their plans in concrete, instead of the other way about. Their goals are easily changed or abandoned, if the going gets tough, but their approach or method remains rigid. In other words, they will try a certain amount of times to achieve their goal, but if it doesn't happen by then, they quit. That is not the way to success and it is certainly not the way to develop belief in yourself, because what happens the next time you are faced with a challenge? Subconsciously you will be telling yourself, "If gets too tough, I'm out of here!" And guess what happens to your self image? It takes a nose-dive. Your self confidence also begins to plummet, unless you decide to make a stand, and keep your goals in concrete. If you fail to reach your goals, you simply reset them and keep trying, no matter how long it takes. You can alter your technique or strategy as much as you want, but don't give up on your goal. Adopt the "I will until" attitude.

When a boxer steps into the ring, his goal is to beat his opponent. Even if he gets knocked down, or is being totally outclassed, his goal remains the same. When he sits down in the corner, between rounds, his manager might advise him to change his strategy or technique, but his goal is still to beat his opponent. Imagine how absurd it would be if the boxer said to his manager, "I don't want to change my tactics; I'll just keep doing what I'm doing. But I don't think I've got a hope in hell of beating this guy, can you bring on a different opponent instead?" Now, we might laugh at how ridiculous that sounds, but many of us do the exact same thing in our daily lives. We find the goal 'too tough' so we try something different instead.

I've seen this happen in so many different areas in people's lives. People start keeping fit or go on diets, and they give up because it seems like hard work, or too much effort. People buy a set of weights, use them for a few months and end up selling them. In network marketing, especially, I have seen many people leave and get duped into some 'get rich quick scheme' which they were told would make them more money, quicker and easier. In my opinion, this negative attitude is usually caused by one of two things ; either, they are trying to get something for nothing, or they simply don't believe that they have what it takes to succeed, so they look for something 'easier'. The problem is that, what they are looking for doesn't exist.

Personally, I've never seen anyone who quit the business, make it in another venture which 'seemed easier'. Why? Because they're usually lazy and haven't developed success habits. And until they do develop them, and change their attitude, success will always elude them, and they will be chasing fool's gold.

Do you believe you will reach your goals? Your answer to that will determine whether you achieve them or not. If you don't believe you will, then you are defeated before you start, but if you do believe, then "Everything is possible for him who believes" (Mark 9: 23)

Finally, I'd just like to share with you, a little poem I came across, some time ago, which I thought was typical of how so many of us defeat ourselves, by our own negative thinking. It's called 'IF'

IF

If you think you are beaten, you are
If you think you dare not, you don't
If you'd like to win, but think you can't
It's almost certain you won't
If you think you'll lose, you've lost
For out of the world we find
Success begins with a fellows will-
It's all in the state of mind
If you think you're outclassed, you are

BELIEF and your INNER VOICE

You've got to think high to rise
You've got to be sure of yourself before
You can ever win a prize
Life's battles don't always go
To the stronger or faster man
But sooner or later, the man who wins
Is the one who thinks he can.

(Anonymous)

CHAPTER 6

BELIEVE IN OTHER PEOPLE

Why was the last chapter so important? Because it is impossible to believe in other people if you don't believe in yourself. That's why there is so much emphasis on the need to believe in yourself. Only when you have developed a good self image, can you help other people to do the same. How can a person who lacks confidence, possibly help and inspire other people? They can't. The Bible says "If a blind man leads a blind man, both will fall into a pit" (Mat 15: 14) No-one would believe in a person if they didn't believe in themselves. Therefore it takes someone with confidence to lead and inspire other people.

Imagine going along to a seminar to learn about personal development, and the speaker was a bit jittery, had a poor self image, and didn't believe in himself. Yet he was there to teach you how to develop self confidence. Would you listen to him? Probably not. Would you go back? Probably not.

A person who believes in themselves finds it easy to believe in others, even if the other person lacks confidence and doesn't believe in themselves. A successful person knows that whatever one man is capable of, so is another. They also know that confidence can be developed by any human being on planet earth. Why? Because they've already done it. Part of believing in yourself is having an inner voice which says "I can", instead of "I can't". When your inner voice says "I can", you can help other people to believe they can.

Developing belief in yourself is not an overnight process, neither is it an event. It is a lifelong process of facing your fears and controlling what goes into your mind. For only then, can we know the way. And only then, can we show the way. Only then do we gain confidence, and realise that God put the seeds of greatness in everyone, without exception.

In a similar way, believing in other people is also a process, which requires patience, and often forgiveness. People will mess up from time to time, just as we ourselves mess up. Why? Because we are all human. There's not a human being on this planet today, that doesn't occasionally do something foolish.

I don't care how successful they are, or what title they have. In fact having a title is sometimes a handicap. There was only one Person who ever walked on this planet without making a mistake, and He was here more than 2000 years ago.

People might do things, unintentionally that upset you, and you might be tempted to think "How dumb!" or "How foolish!" But don't be so quick to judge. Realise that they are learning, just like you. Realise that you were once at their level. Realise that mistakes are normal, and are also part of the learning curve. Without mistakes, there can be no progress, because failure is part of success. I can honestly say that I have learned more from my failures than I have from my successes. Without these 'failures' success would have been impossible, because each 'failure' taught me something valuable. So, allow people time to grow, and allow them the freedom to fail. That doesn't mean that you don't correct their behaviour, it simply means it should be done in a way which is tactful and encouraging, with the purpose of correcting rather than rebuking.

Often when I feel the need to correct someone, I use the feel, felt, found approach. I say "I know how you feel, I felt the same way, but here's what I found......." And I've never come across anyone yet, who's been offended by that. It's a far more human approach than saying "Do as I say because I say so" which is the approach that many bosses use. Such an approach usually causes resentment and only leads to a lack of enthusi-asm and a drop in productivity.

In my opinion, 'fear motivation' is not the best form of motivation, and should only be used as a last resort. I prefer to use 'reward motivation' as far as possible. In other words focus on the benefits of doing something well, as opposed to the consequences of doing something badly.

PRACTICE WITHOUT PRESSURE

We never want to create a situation where people are afraid of making mistakes, for fear of being criticised, or even humiliated. Sadly, this happens all too often, especially in the workplace, and is a direct reflection of either arrogance, poor management, or a lack of knowledge (or sometimes all three). Some people don't realise that people perform much better without pressure, or fear of reprisals. If you can take that pressure off them, and let them realise that they won't get punished or shouted at for making mistakes, then their performance will increase dramatically. You can't have fun doing something if fear of being reprimanded is at the back of your mind. If people are afraid to do something because of fear of consequences, then performance, innovation and creativity will be stifled. As a result, productivity goes down, along with morale. But when people are having fun doing something, they will perform better automatically because they have enthusiasm. When people are enthusiastic, they have more energy and productivity goes up.

Fear of making mistakes and putting people under pressure to perform, actually causes people to make more mistakes. Why? Because subconsciously, the thought of making mistakes is at the back of their mind. You cannot focus on the opposite of an idea. If you are trying not to make a mistake, then your focus will be on the subject of mistakes and this is what you will attract. Instead, the focus should be only on doing the job well, and this can only be done when the fear of mistakes is completely removed from your mind, and replaced with creativity, innovation and doing the job well. Good managers allow people to fail, without fear of punishment, but poor managers use fear of punishment as motivation to perform.

When people mess up, or disappoint you, instead of getting angry, stay calm and have faith in their ability to improve. It's not that the ability isn't there. It's just a case of bringing it out. But whether they develop the ability depends a lot on what kind of reinforcement they get. If they get positive reinforcement and encouragement, there's a high chance they're going to improve. But if they get criticism, ridicule and put-down comments, they probably won't even want to perform, just to spite you.

It's a bit like planting a seed. If you water it, fertilise it and nurture it, then one day it will turn into a beautiful flower. But suppose you gave it poison and put it in a horrible environment? There's no way it would turn into a beautiful flower, because it would probably die. But does that mean it didn't have the potential to become a beautiful flower? No, the potential was there all the time, but it never blossomed because of how you treated it. The seed can go either way, but it all depends on the input it receives. People are similar.

It's a well known psychological fact that people usually rise to the expectations we have of them. This is especially true of children. It's very sad that some children are told by teachers and parents that they are no good at certain things and will never amount to much. To me, that is almost a criminal offence! Who gave us the right to judge someone like that? Who are we to label someone as such, when an Almighty God believes in them? Who do we think we are? Tell a child they're stupid and they're likely to stay that way, but tell them that they're clever and they're improving every day and they're likely to behave that way as well. Either way we are fertilising the seed. Remember, the seed will go either way!

DON'T OVER-PROTECT PEOPLE

Some people can't stand the thought of allowing people who are close to them to fail, but that's the only way they are going to develop their suit of armour. If failure is a necessary part of success for us, then it is also a necessary part of success for them. I don't mean you sit idly by while someone makes a foolish mistake that you could have helped them to avoid, I mean advise them as best as you can, tell them what you recommend and then allow them to make their own decisions. You cannot force someone to do something but you can tell them beforehand what you recommend, and the potential benefits of doing it. You can also tell them what you advise them not to do, and the potential consequences of doing so, so that they are aware of it before they make their own decision.

Once you have advised them to the best of your ability, you just have to let them get on with it. You have got to allow them the freedom to fail. They may take your advice or they may not. But at least, if they go against what you advised, you can always say "I told you so, but you wouldn't listen". Don't say "You idiot! What did I tell you?" That is the worst thing you can possibly do, and will cause them to resent you. If you say to someone "You idiot!" you don't define them, you define yourself. You might think you are defining them but you are actually demonstrating to the world that you are a certain type of person by your words. People define us by our words too. Instead, stay calm and just say politely "I did warn you, didn't I?"

In networking, we were always taught to give suggestions, not commands, because at the end of the day people will do what they want to do anyway. But they are more likely to listen to you if you make a suggestion, rather than give an order and sound like a boss. Often in the business, we would give people advice and they would still do the opposite. However, many of them, after realising their way didn't work, would come back and say they wanted to try our way. But we didn't get annoyed with them or criticise them because we had done (and probably still do) the same thing ourselves. We just politely smiled and said "That's great", and then proceeded to work out a plan of action. So we had to allow people the freedom to fail, because out of their failures they would have learned something valuable, which would have contributed to their overall success. As a result of these 'detours' they would also have been a bit wiser, because of what they had experienced. In other words, they would have learned what not to do.

Some people over-protect their children, and sometimes their partners. As a result, they deny them the ability to develop self confidence. They don't want them to experience any of the 'hurts' in life so they try to shelter them, and in doing so, they never let them develop the ability to stand on their own two feet. They think they are helping them, but in actual fact, they are doing them the biggest dis-service they could possibly imagine. Because if these people suddenly found themselves in a situation where they had to fend for themselves, they wouldn't have a clue what to do. It would be like being pushed in at the deep end and not knowing how to swim. They are also robbing them of the opportunity to become confident, for it is only by experiencing failures and hurts that you can become confident. I'm sorry but there is no other way. You will normally find that the people with the most confidence and who are emotionally strongest are the people who have been through the most. And I'm talking about the tough times as well as the good times. But if these people had been 'sheltered' then they would never be where they are now.

Take for example, the case of Mr. Smith. Mr Smith does everything for his wife because he wants to protect her. He doesn't involve her in any of the decisions, in case she does something wrong and she feels bad. Instead, he takes care of everything. He works out all the finances and gives her 'pocket money'. She never has to think, because everything is done for her. He doesn't let her drive, in case she has a wreck or damages the car. He thinks he is doing her a favour. But what about her level of confidence? Actually, she hardly has any confidence at all, because this has been the pattern for most of their marriage. She's never had the chance to gain confidence because she has never had the chance to experience anything. Part of gaining self confidence and developing belief in yourself is found in the thrill of overcoming obstacles. When you achieve something you thought you couldn't, or overcome something which seemed insurmountable, your self belief and confidence soar to a new level. This new level changes your self-image (who you believe you are) and your inner voice is now one of "I can" instead of "I can't".

It doesn't matter how badly you mess up, it still contributes to your overall level of confidence, as long as you persist and learn from it. How could a boxer ever become a good boxer if he was prevented from going into the ring during training sessions? He couldn't. He has to go into the ring during training and accept the fact that he's sometimes going to come off second best. That's the only way forward. And so it is in life. We have to be willing to be hurt and we have to allow other people to be put into situations where they could also get hurt. The risk of being 'hurt' could be emotional, or physical, but we can't run away from it, because that's life.

DON'T PRE-JUDGE

Never pre-judge people. Not only is it wrong, but it can also be expensive. You wouldn't like it if someone pre-judged you and decided how much potential you had. Would you? Then why do it to someone else? We don't know how someone else ticks. We don't know what their dreams or desires are, or what motivates them. We don't know how badly they would love to improve their lifestyle and get out of the rut they are in.

In network marketing, very often the people I thought would definitely be interested in the concept weren't and the people I thought wouldn't be interested were. My 'assumptions' were proved wrong time and time again. Many of the people I signed up, were people I almost never contacted, either through fear, or because I had simply decided in my own mind that they were going to say "No". The problem was that I was pre-judging people and mentally, I was deciding for them. As a result, I would have people on my list that I decided I would never approach, either because they were already wealthy or because I thought they wouldn't be interested in the idea. How foolish! Why? Because I was assuming.

It can often feel intimidating to call someone about a business idea when they are making about ten times the amount you are. You feel uncomfortable and you start telling yourself things like "Who am I to call them? They won't listen to me! Besides, they're already rich". You assume they are going to laugh at you and tell you what a load of rubbish it sounds. So instead of calling them, you put them on your 'chicken list' (the list you will keep for evermore but never actually call) Instead of getting out of your comfort zone and calling them, you decide to call people who you feel comfortable with. You call the people you think 'need' the business. You tell yourself "Why call the guy making a six figure income? He doesn't need it. I'll call Joe down the road because he's broke and he needs the money more than they do". You might even start to put yourself down and say "Who am I to approach a guy making ten times the amount I am? I'm just a ditch digger and he's an airline pilot" But if you approach someone with this attitude, this is the response you will likely attract because it will come across to them, almost like a sixth sense. It will come across in your tone of voice, your posture and you level of belief.

Can you see how important it is to believe in yourself? If you don't believe in yourself, then other people won't believe in you and you won't get the results. Let me explain why those two reasons for not calling someone are foolish:

1. He's already wealthy

We don't know what someone else's financial situation is. We might think we do but we don't. Yes they may have the cars, the house, the holidays etc, but they might not own the car. They might be up to their eyeballs in debt, just to look good. They might be paying it off for the next five years. Regarding the house and the holidays, they might just be struggling to make ends meet. Maybe they don't have a penny left over, once they've had their holidays. Maybe they don't save and they are in danger of losing their home, should one of them get made redundant. Maybe they are walking a financial tight-rope and they are just praying for an opportunity to have financial security. Maybe they hate their jobs and would love an opportunity to get out of it.

Also, offering someone a business opportunity has nothing to do with who 'needs' money the most. Forget about who needs the money the most. People who are already successful are usually the best prospects because they have already proven that they have a good work ethic. That's why they are successful. Often, they are the most ambitious and will welcome a chance to look at another opportunity. Whereas, people at the lower end of the income ladder usually lack the ambition that successful people have. Not all the time, but most of the time.

2. Assuming they're going to say "No"

Assuming is a major human fault because it has no basis of truth, and can lead us into making bad decisions. Assuming can cause soldiers in battle to get killed. It can cause car crashes if we assume wrongly. It can cause business failures if we assume we know the facts but don't. Assuming can cause all kinds of trouble, just because we failed to find out the facts.

It can also be expensive for us, if we assume that people are not going to be interested in our business idea. Why? because they might be the very people that do it. Not only that, but if you don't contact them, someone else will. Then how will you feel if they show up in someone else's group? All because you assumed they wouldn't be interested. So, what's the best way to find out if they are interested? Contact them and ask them! Then you will know the facts. Yes, you might occasionally get chewed out, or come across a rough customer, but it's still better to know the facts, and it also helps to build your suit of armour.

On the subject of assuming, I remember hearing a story about a man who was driving in the middle of the country when his car got a puncture. It was about 3am, and it was pitch black, in the middle of nowhere. There was only one problem, he didn't have a jack. He had a torch and a spare tyre, but he didn't have a jack or a mobile phone. (I don't think they had mobile phones at that time) There were no houses or towns for miles and he was on his own. He waited to see if there were any other passing vehicles, but because it was a remote area, no other vehicles came. He wondered what to do. He scanned the horizon and saw nothing. No lights, no buildings. Nothing. Suddenly he remembered, about 4 miles back he passed a farmhouse, but it was 3am. He couldn't go to someone's door at 3am, especially when he was a total stranger. Or could he?

After giving it some thought, he decided he had no other option. So he started walking back, hoping they might sympathise with him. Carefully he headed towards the farmhouse, shining his torch on the road. Suddenly he began to have an inner dialogue with himself. He imagined how angry the farmer would be when he rang the doorbell in the middle of the night, asking for a loan of a jack. He visualised him shouting and cursing from the upstairs window, saying "What the hell do you want at this time of night? Who are you anyway? I don't know you!" Then he began to wonder if the farmer might have guard dogs. He might set his dogs on him, and look upon him as a thief or a trespasser. "Maybe the farmer has a shotgun. I might get shot!"

For the whole duration of the trip back to the farmhouse he imagined the worst possible scenario happening, to the extent that he had almost convinced himself it was fact. His subconscious was now responding emotionally to his own thoughts and was ready for a showdown. Instead of visualising what he wanted to happen, he was picturing what he didn't want to happen. Suddenly he could make out the silhouette of the farmhouse and all the lights were off. As he approached the house and was walking up the driveway, he saw someone open an upstairs window and lean out. Before the person in the house could even say a word, he (the driver) shouted up "If that's the way you feel mate, you can stick your jack!" And he turned round and walked away.

The point of the story? Never assume! Because if we assume wrongly, our subconscious starts to respond emotionally to what is imagined, and will create negative situations and events un-necessarily. That farmer might have been a friendly person and was opening his window to see if that guy needed any help. But he (the driver) was never going to know that, because he had already decided in his own mind that the farmer was unfriendly. Therefore he probably created a negative situation un-necessarily, all because of his own negative beliefs. He could have just as easily imagined a positive outcome, if he had told himself different things. He could have imagined the farmer being sympathetic and offering to help. He could have prayed to God that he wouldn't get shot or bitten by dogs, and that the farmer would be understanding.

Some people might argue that no matter what the driver told himself, this wouldn't change the response of the farmer. Well, the important thing to realise is that the inner dialogue the driver had with himself, all the way back to the farmhouse was all-important, because this would determine his own state of mind. His state of mind then had the power to attract the physical counterpart. Depending on what he told himself, his state of mind would either be positive or negative. In this case it was negative. Remember that whatever thoughts dominate your mind, you will attract to yourself in actual physical reality (more commonly known as the 'law of attraction'). Some people might not agree with this philosophy but my own personal view is that he would have most likely attracted that which reflected his state of mind. You need to believe the best about people, unless, of course, they prove otherwise. But not until that point, otherwise you will be assuming.

TRUST

If you are going to believe in people, then trust has to be part of the equation. If you don't trust, then doubt and suspicion automatically become the dominant emotions. Trust transcends those negative emotions and although it places you in a position where you could get hurt, it also opens the door for even greater opportunities. Without trust, there can be no advancement because your own negative thinking will destroy any chance of it. It is far better to trust and get hurt, than not to trust and never get hurt. Why? Because you won't always get hurt. Sometimes the trust pays off and can lead to amazing things. But had you never trusted, you would never have made that breakthrough, or discovery. If you do get hurt, then not only does it strengthen you, but usually there is something valuable to be learned. When you trust someone, you are actually in an all-win situation; it is either going to pay off, or you are going to learn something valuable. My philosophy is to trust people, unless they prove otherwise. If a person then proves themselves untrustworthy, then that is a different story, but not until that point should someone be looked upon as untrustworthy. Ralph Waldo Emerson said "Trust men and they will be true to you; treat them greatly and they will show themselves great". Often, when you trust people, they will be trustworthy. They don't want to let you down because you have given them a high reputation to live up to and they don't want to spoil it. I'm not saying that is always the case, but often it is.

Often you hear people saying that they're never going to trust anyone again in a relationship because they've been hurt. But that is really quite foolish because you cannot say that everyone is the same. Every person is unique, and every situation is unique, so how can you possibly compare, or stereotype? Trust doesn't mean that you throw caution to the wind and take foolish chances, but it should never inhibit you in such a way that it blocks any possibility for advancement.

I am reminded of the true story of a couple who were struggling to trust each other. For the sake of the example, I will call them Angela and Dave. Angela had just met Dave and they were very keen on each other. But the problem for Angela was that although she was very keen on him, her parents disapproved of him and refused to meet him, which hurt her. Some of her other relatives were also saying negative things about him and trying to put her off. To make matters worse, she had a close male friend, who also wanted a date with her, but she wasn't interested, she only wanted him as a friend. When he found out she was seeing Dave, he was extremely disappointed and tried to put her of him too. This 'male friend' knew Dave and started to tell her some negative things about him. He said that Dave had cheated on his wife in a previous marriage and would probably do the same thing to her. When Angela continued to see Dave, this 'male friend' stopped talking to her. She felt that everyone, including her own family was turning against her because she was seeing Dave. Finally, in her despair, she called me, and explained the situation. I asked her if all these accusations were based on truth or opinion? She said she wasn't sure if they were true or not. So I said "Then take no counsel of them" I also said that even if these things were true, it doesn't mean Dave is like that now. People can change. Therefore I wouldn't allow the past to control the future, especially when there is no evidence or proof to back it up. I said "You really need to decide for yourself whether to keep seeing him or not, but if you want my advice, do what you really want to do. Don't do things to try and please other people. If they don't approve, that's their problem."

She decided to keep seeing him. But the other problem, especially for Angela was her suspicion and doubt. Her previous relationships had been a mess and her self image badly affected, as a result of criticism and put-down comments. Some of her previous partners had been unfaithful to her and this caused her to be suspicious about Dave un-necessarily. Suspicion constantly dominated her mind. Dave sometimes worked far away from home, and every time when she phoned and he didn't answer, she wondered if he might be with someone else. When she did finally get an answer, she would be short with him and give him a ticking off.

Sometimes when Dave was meant to phone her, he wouldn't call until late on or sometimes the next day. This caused Angela to be suspicious. But the truth was, because he worked for himself, he was often in middle of a job, and wasn't always able to phone at the exact time. When he did phone he was also suspicious of her because he knew how pretty she was, and was convinced that other guys would be trying to date her. As a result, he would often make sarcastic comments to her on the phone. As a result of all this, two people were destroying a perfectly good relationship un-necessarily.

I pointed out to Angela that her suspicion was based on something which was imagined, and not necessarily real. I said, "For all you know, he might be innocent. Then, how will Dave feel if you are accusing him of things he hasn't done? How would you feel if someone was accusing you, and you were innocent? You have to give people the benefit of the doubt. If not, then you could destroy a perfectly good relationship" I recommended that she flush all these negative thoughts and act as though he was completely trustworthy, unless he proved otherwise. As a result she would also alleviate herself of a huge amount of anxiety and stress, which would give her peace of mind. I told her that every time a negative thought came into her mind about Dave, to flush it immediately and replace it with something positive. I told her that there's no point worrying or being suspicious anyway, because all the worrying about it, isn't going to change a thing, so she may as well be happy about it. She finally agreed to stop thinking that way. As a result, her attitude towards Dave changed and they started to get on better. I couldn't help but remind her of the famous Elvis Presley record "Suspicious Minds" when Elvis says "We can't go on together with suspicious minds" And how true that is, because suspicion will destroy a relationship.

I also told her that her attitude of not wanting to fall out with people because of Dave was causing her more grief than she could possibly imagine. She needed to flush that attitude and replace it with the attitude "I'll do what I believe is right, and if you don't agree, that's too bad. I won't fall out with you, but if you fall out with me, that's your problem, not mine" I also gave her a list of affirmations to practice daily, which I have listed here:

I make up my own mind about people

I take no notice of gossip or criticism. I just let it bounce off me

I base my decisions on facts, not rumours

I am here to please God, not people

God gives me wisdom and strength, therefore I make good decisions

Dave is faithful and so am I

Everyone is innocent unless they prove otherwise, therefore I trust everyone

The past doesn't matter, neither theirs or mine. Every day is a new beginning

All that matters is now

The past has no bearing on the future

Today is a gift. That's why its called the present

Because I trust people, they love me for it and they are trustworthy

It doesn't matter what other people think, I believe in myself and I make good decisions

When I make a decision, I stand by it

LET PEOPLE KNOW YOU BELIEVE IN THEM

It is one thing to believe in people, but it is another to communicate this to them. By telling someone you believe in them not only will they love you for it, but they will also want to perform just to please you. When they realise you have high expectations for them, they won't want to destroy that, by letting you down. So if you believe in someone, and their ability to do something, tell them.

I remember some time ago I was asked to do a speech at someone's birthday party in front of about 50 to 100 people. Although I appreciated being asked, my first thought was "Hold on a minute, that will be extremely uncomfortable for me". Even although I knew most of the people who would be there, including many relatives, the fear factor was still there, because it would be out of my comfort zone. Then my inner voice came into play. Initially my inner voice said "How can I get out of it?" Then I realised the damage I was doing to myself, so I began to tell myself "You need to face your fears and practice getting out of your comfort zone, if you want to be successful" In other words I had to do it. I also had to take control, and replace the negative inner voice with the positive inner voice. So I said "No problem, just tell me what you want me to say, and I'll go to work on it right away".

But the thing that appealed to me most was what they said next, and how they expressed their belief in me. In fact, at that point in my life, they might have expressed more belief in me than I had in myself. They said "I'd like you to do a speech for us at the party because I think you'd be good at it" How could I possibly let someone down who had such high expectations for me? Of course I would do it. The decision was now made. The only thing to be decided was exactly what I would say, how many times a day I would practice, and how I would overcome the fear factor. It was not a case of 'if' I would face the fear, because that had already been decided. It was a case of 'how' I would deal with it. I decided that I would do everything possible, and use every trick in the book, to perform as well as I could, because that person believed in me. I probably practiced giving that speech, in the privacy of my own room, more times than I normally would have, all because that person believed in me.

PEOPLE CAN CHANGE

We must never find ourselves in the position of 'labelling people'. We must never say things like "Your wasting your time on them" or "Don't bother with him, he's hopeless" or "Forget about him, do you know what he done not too long ago? Let me tell you…….." Remember, the past is over and we shouldn't be using it as a yardstick to judge people. I'm not saying we should disregard what people do, but if a person has changed their ways, then it should be forgotten. We must always bear in mind that the same person is able to change. Some people are willing to change and some are not. But it's not where a person's been that matters' it's where they are going and what they are like now that counts. If God continually used our past against us, then none of us would ever get to heaven. We would ALL be eternally consigned to the lake of fire. God is ALWAYS willing to forgive what we have done, as long as we repent and confess our sins to Him. If God is willing to forget about our past, what right do we have to say that a certain person is no good because they have behaved a certain way in the past. If we do that, then we are playing 'God' and acting as Judge, something we have no right to do.

The apostle Paul considered himself 'the least of the apostles' because of his anti-Christian background. Before Paul was converted, he was guilty of persecuting Christians and having them stoned to death. After his conversion, he himself was willing to be persecuted for the very things he had persecuted others for. "For I am the least of the apostles and do not even deserve to be called an apostle, because I persecuted the church of God. But by the grace of God I am what I am" (1 Cor 15 :

9-10)

Miracles can and do happen, therefore we should always keep an open mind. We should always believe in a **person's** ability to change. People can surprise us. Often, the least likely people can be people who change the most. This doesn't mean that they will, but the potential is there, and always will be. If they don't change, it's not that they are not able to, it's because they choose not to. Change is a choice. The Bible says "Therefore, if anyone is in Christ, he is a new creation; the old has gone, the new has come!" (2 Cor 5: 17) So keep the faith, not only in others, but in yourself!

If my sponsor hadn't believed in me, and decided not to contact me to look at the MLM business concept, then you wouldn't be reading this book just now. It was only as a result of the training system and being willing to change, that I was able to write a book. If I hadn't started reading these books, I would probably still be in the failure mode of thinking, and in the same old rut I used to be in. I actually used to hate reading. But I thank God today that my sponsor contacted me. You know what a rut is don't you? It's just a grave with both ends knocked out.

I believe in you and I've never even met you. How can I say that? Because God created you, and God doesn't create people to fail. Neither does He create inferior products. You are a human being with God-given abilities, and you have the same capacity as anyone else to become great. If you don't believe what I've just said, keep reading daily and never stop. Just fifteen minutes every day and eventually you will start to believe what I've just said. Remember, if you don't believe what I've just said it's not that it's not true, it's just that you don't 'believe' it's true. The problem lies in your thinking and books will change your thinking.

BELIEVE IN EVERYONE BUT WAIT FOR NO-ONE

Although we should believe in everyone, we shouldn't be sitting around waiting on them either. Our time is valuable as well as theirs, and if they don't want to do anything, then move on and find someone else. Don't give up on them, but don't wait for them either. Let them know that the door is always open, but if they're not ready just now, you're not hanging around. If they come back to you some time later, that is fine. Believe in them, but don't wait on them.

In networking many people including myself were guilty of what is called 'hatching people'. That means, you might have twenty good people in your group, but there's this one guy who you are convinced is better than all the rest put together. So, regardless of how interested he is, you put practically all your time and effort into this one guy, in the hope that he's going to tear the business up. Then eventually he disappoints you by saying he's not really interested anymore. Then you're on a real downer, because not only has he said he's not going to do it, but you've wasted all that time and effort over the last few weeks, or maybe months, while practically ignoring all your other people. But is that his fault? No! it's your fault! There's nothing wrong with not being interested, that's his choice. But maybe you put him off. Maybe the pressure was too much. Maybe you were phoning too much, talking too much or being too pushy? Or maybe you were acting desperate and he could sense it.

One of the best pieces of advice I ever got was that people don't want get in business with you, if they think you need them. People can tell if you're desperate, because it leaks out in your body language and your words. Remember, you don't need any 'one' person. There are millions of people, so why act desperate over one? If they're not interested or it isn't a good time for them, move on! Don't sit around waiting for them, and don't act as though you need them. Keep believing in them, and let them know the door is open, but don't wait for them. Let them chase you.

That's another thing you need to avoid, is chasing people. Sometimes if a person says they're interested but it's not the right time for them, we end up calling them back at a later date. Often they're still too busy and we arrange to call them in another couple of months. Then what are we doing? We are chasing them. And you don't want to get in a position where you are running after people. Its not good posture. Its far better to have them call you back. After wasting much valuable time chasing people in this manner, eventually I would say to them "If this isn't a good time for you just now, that's fine, here's my number, you call me when its more convenient" and that way I could move on to the next person on my list. Psychologically I could forget about them, unless they called me.

I'm not trying to sound negative, but the vast majority of them never called. Why? Because, in my opinion, they were time wasters who just didn't want to say no. Instead of 'offending people' by saying 'No' they would rather give you the run-around for weeks on end and waste your valuable time. The point I'm trying to make is that just because I chose not to chase them, didn't mean I didn't believe in them. It just meant I was letting them chase me. I also found that having them phone me, instead of me phoning them, was a valuable screening process. If they were serious, then they would phone. If they didn't phone then they weren't serious. I also found that I was more productive because I was never in the position of waiting on this 'one guy'. I was always on the move, always looking to the next person.

DON'T POVERTY-THINK FOR PEOPLE

Sometimes we are guilty of thinking we know another person's financial situation, and we assume things and try to make financial decisions for them. This usually becomes a problem when we assume they are broke, rather than assume they are wealthy. Sometimes we will say things like "It would be great to invite Joe to the seminar but he's on a low income and I don't think he would be able to afford it. So I won't bother asking him".

As a result of that mentality, we deny Joe the very opportunity that could improve his financial situation. And it's not his fault, it's our fault! Why? Because we have assumed we know his financial situation. Yes, maybe he is on a low income, but that doesn't mean he doesn't have the money, or isn't able to come up with the money. Neither is it our right to decide for him. For all we know, Joe might have thousands of pounds in another bank account, or he might be able to borrow the money from a family member. Maybe he has things he could sell and would dearly love to come to the seminar, if given the opportunity. Maybe he has other ventures, as well as his full time job. We don't know!

So, what is the answer? The answer is, act as though he has got the money unless he tells you otherwise. If he hasn't got the money, let him tell you that. Otherwise act as though he is going. When you promote the seminar to him, don't say things like "I know it's a lot of money" or "I know you might not be able to afford it". Forget about all that, that is negative thinking! When you think negatively, you get negative results! You also plant negative thoughts in his mind. Instead, promote the seminar, tell him how important it is, and how it will improve his financial situation. Tell him how wise an investment it is, and how the long-term return will far outweigh the cost. Tell him about the quality of the speakers, and that it will be a life-changing experience. Tell him that he can't afford not to go.

Did you notice something about what I've just said? I have focused on all the positive aspects of going to the seminar, like the benefits which will come from it, but someone who poverty-thinks for other people doesn't see any of that. Instead they focus only on the negatives. They focus on how much the person will be out of pocket, and how awkward it will be for them to get time off work. They might even focus on how difficult it is for them to get a babysitter and stuff like that. In other words, they virtually make the person's mind up for them, and base whether they will ask them or not, on what they assume to be true. Big mistake! The key is to ask everyone, without exception and to promote it to everyone. People will soon let you know if there is a problem.

Many times I've promoted a seminar to people and subconsciously I was thinking "As soon as I mention the price, it will put them off" and it's amazing how many times I was proved wrong. Many of them bought their tickets and went to the seminar, without complaining about the price. The problem was 'my' negative thinking, not theirs. Occasionally some people said they couldn't make it, for whatever reason, but it was never because I planted the negative thoughts in their minds, by saying negative things. You've got to think positive thoughts before you speak positive words. If you're thinking negative thoughts, you will probably speak negative words. Thinking always precedes words. The thought comes first, then the words (or actions, as it may be). Think positive thoughts and you will do positive things and get positive results.

CONDEMN THE BEHAVIOUR, NOT THE PERSON

If we are to believe in other people, we need to see them as they can be, not just as they are. Everyone, no matter how they behave just now, has the potential to become great. Everyone, regardless of how they act just now, has the seeds of greatness within them. It is vitally important to make the distinction between the behaviour and the person. For example, if you say someone is a fool, you are condemning the person, but if you say "That person acted foolishly" you are condemning the behaviour. You are then condemning the act instead of the 'actor'.

This doesn't mean that we should ignore someone's behaviour or fail to discipline them. Of course we need to have discipline, and sometimes punishment, as the case may be. But at the same time, we should also believe in a person's ability to improve. Psychologically we must always keep that door open. After all, God constantly keeps it open for us! But if we fail to see someone as a person who is capable of improving, they probably never will. If for example a child is labelled as a bad child, they will probably continue to be bad. Why? Because if they hear you saying that repeatedly, it will picked up by their subconscious mind, and this will be the image they have of themselves. The image they feel you have of them is the image they will adopt for themselves, and they will more than likely live up to it.

Psychologists tell us that it is virtually impossible to act inconsistently with the way we see ourselves. That's why a child who sees themselves as bad will probably continue to be bad, because it is consistent with their self image. But start telling them they are intelligent and there's a good chance they will become intelligent to avoid disappointing you.

If the image they have of themselves is a 'bad person' they will probably continue to be bad, unless the cycle is broken and replaced with an image of a good person. Only when the image is changed will the behaviour change. Therefore you need to give people as much positive reinforcement as possible. A person who tries to change their behaviour through sheer will-power is trying to pit the tiny conscious against the mighty subconscious. It takes a lot of mental effort and doesn't usually get them very far. This is doing things the hard way.

The easiest and most effective way to change a person's behaviour is when the self image is changed first, because then the change in behaviour is effortless and becomes automatic. If for example, a child who had an image of being a bad person developed an image of being a good person, they would find it easier to act good because this behaviour would now be in alignment with their self image. They now believe they are good, therefore it is second nature to act well. But it would be difficult and feel out of place for someone who believed they were bad, to act good, since they weren't used to it and it would also be inconsistent with their self image. Therefore the new behaviour would probably be short lived and soon rejected by their subconscious mind, as they would feel 'out of place' acting good, while they believed they were bad.

What I am trying to say is work on developing a person's self image, if you want their behaviour to change. This might sound like a paradox, but if you want their behaviour to change, forget about their behaviour. That will take care of its self in due course, if you help them develop their self image. Don't expect someone to suddenly start acting good, out of the blue. Instead help to build them up. Start telling them you believe in them. Tell them they've got great potential, but they're just not using it. Tell them you are surprised at them acting foolishly, when they are capable of being much better. Thinking 'always' precedes actions. If they sense you believe in them, there's a good chance they will start to believe more in themselves too. Feed them positive books. That will change their self image better than anything else.

If you see someone acting foolishly, try not to see them as a fool. Instead see them as a person with great potential acting foolishly, so that their behaviour is the only thing in question, and not the person themselves. I remember hearing a good example of this when a man and his wife were in a restaurant. They had just ordered their meals and the waiter serving them was a bit rude and impolite. The husband said something to his wife about how rude the waiter was, but instead of criticising him, his wife said "He needs to read a few more books" Although she didn't like his behaviour either, she also believed in his ability to improve. Instead of seeing him as a fool, she saw him as someone with great potential, acting foolishly.

PASS YOUR KNOWLEDGE ON

It is one thing to acquire knowledge, but it is even more rewarding to be able to pass on to other people what you have learned and help them to improve their own lives. It's great to know you can make a positive difference in the lives of other people, especially if they are going through what you've already been through yourself. When you know the way, you can show the way, but only if you've been that way yourself. Other people can benefit from your failures, as well as your successes, by showing them what to avoid, as well as what to do.

Life can be a bit like a minefield. There are hardships and adversity as well as the good times. If we have successfully made it through a particular minefield, and we see less experienced people fumbling their way through it, not knowing which way to go, we can guide them and show them what path to take and what paths to avoid. Then, when these people eventually make it through, they themselves can pass onto others what they have learned. This is when you truly begin to make a difference in the lives of others. When you see other people's lives improve, as a result of what you have taught them, it is truly rewarding. You know that in some small way, you are making a difference in the world. It is when you take your eyes of yourself and put them onto other people, that you are happiest.

Knowledge is only beneficial if it meets two requirements ; firstly, it is acted upon, and secondly, it is shared. If you keep knowledge to yourself, it will eventually die within you. And how can you leave a lasting impression on mankind, or leave a legacy without sharing what you have with other people? You can't!   Not only that, but life isn't much fun, and not very rewarding if you keep things to yourself. You probably won't be very happy either. For true happiness is in the giving, not in the taking.

During World War Two, in the war in the Pacific, I listened to a veteran pilot say that if an American pilot was fortunate enough to complete a certain amount of missions, he was allowed to leave combat duties in order to train new pilots. His valuable experience and skill at having successfully completed so many combat missions was put to maximum use, by passing it onto inexperienced pilots, so that as many people as possible could benefit from it. This also helped the overall war effort, as well as at an individual level. But he went onto say that the Japanese used to keep their pilots out there, until they died. It may have been brave, but it wasn't going to help them win the war. As a result, any skills they had, died with them.

Learn to share your knowledge and experiences with others, and it will come back to you a hundred-fold. If you practice helping other people, you are sowing a seed. Make it a habit and eventually you will reap a harvest. Maybe when you are in need, someone will help you.

Never forget where you came from. I will never forget where I came from. I will never forget the people who have helped me, by giving me a hand up, in my darkest times. I will be forever grateful to people who have spoken with me and advised me on a personal one to one basis. I will be forever grateful to every speaker I have ever heard at a seminar. I will be forever grateful to every business person, pastor or minister I have ever heard on a CD or tape. I will be eternally grateful to every author who has written a life-changing book, and there have been many of them. Some of these people I have met, some I will never meet, yet all have played a part, and all have contributed to my life. They will do the same for you.

"No man is an island"
John Donne (1572-- 1631)

CHAPTER 7

MAKING DECISIONS

Our subconscious mind can be a valuable ally in the decision making process, if we will listen to it. We make decisions each and every day of our lives. Some of these decisions are minor, such as deciding what to wear or what to eat, but at other times we have more important decisions to make, such as dealing with a relationship problem or a financial problem, and sometimes we don't know what to do. But how do we listen to our subconscious you might ask? We do it by listening to our emotions. After all, our emotions come from the subconscious. Some people might call this a 'gut feeling' but it still comes from the subconscious nevertheless.

Sometimes when you are faced with a problem, there are more than just two options. Sometimes there might be four or five options, or possibly more! So how do you decide what to do, when you don't know what to do? Personally I rely more on my subconscious than anything else. Sure I use logic too, but if what I think logically, is in conflict with my emotions, or is causing me to have negative emotions, I rule that choice out immediately. Our conscious minds know very little in comparison to our subconscious minds. The times when I have made the worst decisions is when I have ignored my inner voice (emotions) and carried on regardless. Any decision which causes negative emotions is usually a bad decision. Let us not forget that doubt is a negative emotion. I can only talk from my own experience, but any time I have had a choice to make and I have been in doubt, I found it was better to leave it out. This could have been a choice to do with buying clothes, buying a house, or anything at all for that matter.

For example, sometimes I have bought clothes on impulse, or thought something was a good buy. At the same time I also had to think about it. In other words, I wasn't 100 percent sure I wanted it. The result? It never got worn. It lay on my shelf for months. In the end, I ended up giving it to a charity shop. On the other hand, there have been times when I saw something, and I knew immediately that I wanted it. There was no doubt in my mind, and I didn't have to think about it. The result? I put it on as soon as I bought it and wore it regularly. Now, when I am faced with tough decisions, I think through each option, and I imagine doing it. You get the same emotions by imagining something, as you do when you actually do it, because your subconscious doesn't know the difference between a real experience and one vividly imagined. When I imagine making a decision, I check how this makes me feel emotionally. The option that gives me the best overall feeling is the choice I end up making. Sometimes I have to ignore what I think 'consciously' if my emotions are telling me otherwise. Sometimes, the option I imagine causes me to feel negative right away, in which case, it is immediately ruled out. But other times, one of the options stands out among the rest, and gives me a definite good feeling. This is usually your subconscious guiding you. It has been my experience that it's seldom, if ever, wrong.

I remember when I was looking to buy a house. I had been looking regularly for several months, but each time I saw a house that I liked, I was outbid. Other times there were houses that I couldn't decide whether to put in an offer or not. I was unsure whether to go for it or not, so I remembered the golden rule; 'If in doubt, leave it out'. On hindsight I am glad that I did leave them out. But when I eventually did come across the house I wanted, there was absolutely no doubt in my mind at all. Consciously, I was sure I wanted it. My subconscious was also in agreement because there was no doubt. Instead I just had a definite overall, good feeling about it. Obviously buying a house is a far more serious decision than buying clothes. Therefore, it becomes even more crucial not to be in doubt.

When I have made wrong decisions, and there have been many of them, it has often been because I've been suffering from other negative emotions and possibly stress. When negative emotions are dominating our thinking, it clouds our judgement and causes confusion. This often leads us to making the wrong decision when we think we are making the right decision. The solution? If it is at all possible, wait until you are in a more positive frame of mind before deciding. If for example, you are deciding how to deal with an awkward customer or a co-worker and you are suffering from anger, you will probably say things you may later regret. Better to wait until you are in a more positive frame of mind so that you can think more clearly.

There have been times when I've had to speak to a customer about something confrontational, and I wasn't in the best frame of mind. I was either stressed out or suffering from other negative emotions, such as anger. I wanted to say something there and then, but something deep within me said WAIT! Don't mention it until you are in a better frame of mind. I'm sure glad I did wait, because what I decided to say later on, was completely different from what I was going to say. In fact sometimes when I waited until I was in a better frame of mind, I decided it wasn't even worth bothering about and just forgot about it. But the times when I did say something out of anger or other negative emotions, it leads to regret. And even until this day, there are things I still regret. But I don't dwell on it or beat myself up about it. I have to forgive myself and learn from it.

If you have to make a decision about something immediately, you just have to go with your gut feeling and do what you think is best. If the decision turns out to be a wrong decision, you may have to go through a process of trial and error until you find the right one. This often applies when there are many paths to take and you cannot seem to get a definite gut feeling about any one of them. This is often a painful process, but massively contributes to your self image and your 'suit of armour'. It also takes you closer to your dreams. The willingness to endure such trials separates the winners from the losers, the men from the boys, and the successful from the unsuccessful.

NEVER MAKE A DECISION OUT OF DESPERATION

I remember speaking to someone several years ago who made a decision out of desperation and they regretted it. What happened was that their car had failed its test, and had been deemed un-roadworthy because there was so many things wrong with it.

And economically, it made no sense to repair. They were better off just looking for a new car. The problem was that they needed a car for going to their work and they needed it urgently, or so they thought. Normally they would have spent a bit of time looking at different cars before they bought one. But because they reasoned they didn't have time to do that, they went to the car auctions and bought one there. They didn't really want to do that, but felt they had no choice. (But the truth is, we always have a choice) They bought a car which looked good on the outside, but turned out to be an absolute disaster. There were things wrong with the engine and it didn't even have a spare tyre. One problem after another began to unfold, and he realised he'd been had. In other words it was a total waste of money. Ironically, he even got a puncture on the way home, and had to get a friend to help him out because there was no spare tyre. Eventually, he just had to cut his losses and realise life was teaching him a lesson. Needless to say, he didn't hold on to it very long and vowed never to buy a car at the auctions again. He realised it was far better to have the inconvenience of not having a car, than to buy one out of desperation and buy a whole bunch of problems. He had wasted money on a car, which left him with even less money to buy the next one.

SHOULD I OR SHOULDN'T I?

Obviously when we are making decisions there has to be a fair amount of analysing and brainstorming, while listening to our inner voice at the same time. Logic also plays quite a big part in the decision making process because we have to weigh up the pro's and con's of potential situations. This might seem to contradict what I've just said, but because problems are so numerous, vast and varied, there is not always a definite clear-cut, 'one size fits all' answer. Each problem is unique in character and seriousness.

I've found it helpful when faced with a decision, to ask myself what's the best thing that can happen if I succeed? And what's the worst thing that can happen if I fail? Then I can determine what the risk factor is. In other words, what could I gain? And what have I got to lose? You should never just look at what you could gain and you should never just look at what you could lose. To make an informed decision, you must always look at both, then weigh them up against each other. People who only look at what you could lose are pessimists who never get anywhere in life. People, who only look at what you could gain, but forget about the potential down-side, are living in fantasy land, and are running the risk of losing everything.

For example, when I first got involved in multi level marketing, I wasn't sure whether to pull out or not. I had paid my start up fee, but legally still had six months to pull out and get a refund. My 'friends' and even some family members were trying to put me off. They were saying "Don't get involved!" One of my close friends kept telling me it was no good. Ironically, he wasn't anywhere near financially independent himself, because he worked for a boss and made just enough money to make ends meet. One of my other friends had his own business, selling clothes at the market. He kept telling me to get my money back and use it to buy clothes which I could sell at the market. I must admit, I was tempted to quit and get my money back, but something very deep within me was urging me to carry on with the MLM business, which I think (now) was the Holy Spirit.

Logic was telling me to quit and get my money back, but my inner voice was telling me to press on. I began to weigh up the pros and cons of the MLM business. I thought "What have I got to lose?" The answer came back "Less than £100" Then I thought to myself, I've just seen a potentially life changing opportunity, which is unlike anything I've seen before. Even if I did fail, what's £100? It's certainly not much in terms of risk. But what if the business did work? What could I gain? The answer came back "A hell of a lot more than £100!"

I knew that there were many extremely successful people in MLM, but what really made my mind up, more than the money was the people. I had never been around such positive people before. I had been used to the conventional world, where it was 'dog eat dog' and only the strongest survived. This, more than anything attracted me to the business, and caused me to keep going. I began to think about how critical some of my 'friends' had been, and how I'd been stung in the conventional world. I thought "I'd rather hang around with these people. There's no criticism here! In fact, these people do the opposite. They encourage you and help you!" I decided to follow my inner voice.

I couldn't know for sure what this business held in store for me because there were no guarantees. I just knew that there was virtually no risk, but the potential gain was enormous. Looking back, I know that God played a part in keeping me in the MLM business. I know that God wanted me to change in more ways than one, and He used the support system, within the business to get me to change. I know now, that He also had a plan for me to write books, and it would never have been possible if I hadn't gotten involved in the personal development programme. But here's the point ; God will do the same for you in your own life if you will just listen to His call. "For I know the plans I have for you," declares the Lord, "plans to prosper you and not to harm you, plans to give you hope and a future" (Jer 29:11) Sometimes when you have an inner urge to do something, you just need to step out on faith. But only once you have weighed up the pro's and con's.

BRAINSTORM, THEN TAKE A BREAK

When you are analysing a problem and you don't know what to do, the first thing you need to do is gather as much information about it as possible. Then think it through or discuss it, as the case may be. Sometimes this can be a mental dilemma that goes on for hours, days or even weeks. For example, it could be a career choice or deciding what house to buy. It could be deciding what person to employ, or how to solve a DIY problem at home. It could be absolutely anything. Even then, we are often not quite sure what to do. We think about what the best option is and look at the potential gain and potential downside. But sometimes if we brainstorm too long, it can become counter-productive. Our minds can boggle if we have too much brainstorming without a break. This is sometimes referred to as 'paralysis of analysis'.

There's nothing wrong with having a good long hard brainstorming session, as long as it is followed by a considerable period of switching off. Ironically, it is usually in the 'switching off' period, when we are most relaxed, that we get our best ideas. Thomas Edison bears testimony to that. That's because our subconscious works most effectively when there is no pressure. Otherwise, we can 'jam it' by too much conscious effort, which interferes with subconscious processes. Edison found that he got his best ideas when he was in a drowsy state, almost ready to fall asleep.

Sure we need to brainstorm initially to get the facts, and to provide our subconscious with information, but once our subconscious has adequate information, there should be equal importance placed on switching off afterwards, where we forget about the problem and get on with something else. It is when we are relaxed that our subconscious is working most effectively. Don't think that just because you're watching football or painting a picture, or decorating the house that your subconscious isn't working on the problem. It is! That's what subconscious means; (sub) below the level of consciousness. You can be thinking about one thing (consciously) while your subconscious is working on another. The wheels of your subconscious are always in motion, every day, 24 hours a day, every day of your life. Even when you are sleeping, your subconscious will still be wrestling with the problem. Often people awaken in the morning and realise they have the answer.

I've seen myself get stuck with something, such as writing a manuscript or trying to do something on the computer and something goes wrong and I'm there for ages trying to solve it. If you stay at it too long, often frustration starts to creep in and you become even less effective. At this point you are better to stop, take a break and come back to it later. Then go and do something you enjoy, as this will put you back into a positive frame of mind and will get rid of any frustration. Why not go for a walk or listen to your favourite music, or clean your car?

Often during this break, which can often last the whole day, an idea will come into my mind that I might never have thought of, if I hadn't taken a break.

My frustration would have made creative thinking impossible and would have blocked any possibility of it. Your creativity is at its best when you are in a positive state of mind and you are enjoying yourself. Therefore I would actually have been 'less' effective if I hadn't taken a break. Remember that frustration is a negative emotion, and all negative emotions hinder the workings of your subconscious mind.

BEWARE OF EXTREMES

Sometimes in life people go to the extreme, when making decisions. This can often happen when something bad has happened to them. For example, have you ever heard anyone who has just come out of a difficult relationship say "That's it! I'm staying single the rest of my life! I'm not going out with anyone else again" They might not mean it, and are possibly just venting their frustration. There again, they might mean it! But it is most likely that they just want a nice long break before even thinking about another relationship. Often, they can be emotionally exhausted, or simply worn out and just want some time to recoup and get themselves together.

But we need to realise that life isn't always just clear-cut, black and white. There are also some shades of grey in between. And that goes for any area of life, not just relationships. Instead of saying "I'm not going out with anyone again", you could say "I'm going to be more select in who I go out with in the future. I'm in no rush, but if I happen to meet someone I like, then we can always go out on a date and see how we get on"

Consider the case of Linda; Linda was going to finish with her boyfriend. She had been seeing him almost every night for quite some time, but wasn't sure what to do. She said they weren't getting on as well as they used to. He didn't seem the same person as he used to be. He was a bit more argumentative and had become quite controlling. This was causing a lot of friction, and it also reminded her of the treatment she used to get in previous relationships. So she was going to finish the relationship completely. But a friend suggested to her, "Before you do that, why don't you try a change of tactics first? Instead of going to the extreme, it might just be a little fine tuning that is required. Why not cut down the amount of time you see each other? Instead of seeing each other every night, why not just make it one or two nights a week? Or why not just see him at the weekend, and then absence might make the heart grow fonder?"

She gave this a try and emotionally she felt better, for two main reasons. Firstly she began to realise that deep down, what she wanted was more time to herself, while still being able to see her boyfriend. This was a subconscious desire (positive emotion) that she was consciously unaware of. As a result of going against this desire, her subconscious was responding with negative emotions and she wasn't happy. She realised where she had been going wrong; she was either all-out of a relationship, or all-in. She was either seeing no-one or she was seeing them virtually every night. This caused her to grow tired of them.

But now she realised that there are some shades of grey in between. She could still see them once a week, or possibly twice a week and still have a lot of free time for herself and have time to keep in touch with her friends. Yes, she could have the best of both worlds but she had never thought of it before. But please don't take this the wrong way; I'm not saying marriage is going to the extreme. Not in the slightest. God created marriage and anything God created is good. Marriage is a different situation altogether. I'm talking about ordinary relationships and dating people. But sometimes when we meet someone, we are so emotionally overwhelmed that we can't see the wood for the trees. Our emotions blind us from seeing things clearly, and we don't always see things logically.

The second reason Linda felt better was because at a subconscious level, she didn't really want to lose her boyfriend. Her subconscious 'desire' was to keep him. She just wanted things to improve so that she could be happy. Deep down she was happy that he was still in her life and she hadn't ditched him. As a result, her subconscious responded with positive emotions, and she was happy, because she did what she really desired, rather than call it off.

Any time you go against your true desires, you will experience negative emotions. It has to happen, because desire is a positive emotion and you are doing the opposite of that.

FOLLOW YOUR HEART

When it comes to making important decisions, such as a career choice, it's important to listen to your inner voice and follow what your heart is telling you to do. Don't let logic get in the way of what you really want to do. This is when logic can conflict with emotion (conscious conflicting with subconscious). Some people allow money to dictate what path they will take, at the expense of their happiness. Others allow status, prestige or job title to come first and ignore the quiet inner voice which comes from their heart. As a result, some people are often stuck in jobs they detest, causing high stress levels, all because they put other things before what they really want to do.

When you listen to what your heart is telling you to do, you will be happy. Forget about status or job title. What good is status or a job title if you're not happy? You know what the definition of status is, don't you? That's when you buy things you don't need, with money you haven't got, to impress people you don't like. It reminds me of the story of a couple who were struggling to make ends meet. Mr 'X' was talking about how his wife had been promoted to the head of a new department. The problem was, that because of their low income, and having children to raise, they barely had enough money to put food on the table.

One night she came home, all excited because she had been given a new position which gave her greater responsibility. She had also been given a new title. She felt great about it. When she told her husband, he said "That's great, but what does it mean?" She said "Well I'm now in charge of a whole new department and I've even got my own personal parking space" He said "Yeah, but what does it mean?" She said "Are you talking about money?" He said "Yes, how much of a raise are they giving you?" She said "Well there's no raise, but as you can see, I've got a new title and my position now allows me more influence in decision making" He said "Great, let's eat it"

Now that might sound a bit corny but sadly it's all too true in the workplace today. The problem was that his wife was blinded by status and prestige, instead of looking for opportunities that could create wealth. Deep down, his wife had always longed for a business of her own, but because of negative self talk, and a lack of belief in herself, she had suppressed that desire and traded it for status instead. The problem with status is that no-one really cares but you. You may think other people care about your level of status, but realise they're too busy with their own lives and their own problems to be thinking about you. Why deny yourself what you really want, for the sake of status?

HAVE A MIND OF YOUR OWN

Some people take certain career paths in order to please their parents, rather than do what they really want to do. Sometimes parents can (wrongly) put pressure on their children to go into a certain line of work because of prestige and the 'benefits' it offers. Their parents are usually thinking about 'job title' (I won't say job security, because it doesn't exist anymore) and are often overly concerned about what other people will think. They may pride themselves in conversation when they tell people about their son or daughters job title. As a result, their children are often not truly happy because they are suppressing their own desires. Maybe you are a parent who is reading this, or maybe you are the child, but realise that you are an individual, and you have as much right to choose your own career path as anyone else. Each and every person, parent or child, has the right to be what they want. It would be a very dull and boring world if everyone was simply a miniature clone of their parents.

If you are a parent, you need to accept the fact that your children may well have completely different desires, interests and ambitions from you. When it comes to career choice, you need to respect the wishes of your son or daughter. If you do that, they will love you for it. Better still, encourage them, even if it's something which is totally uninteresting to you. If they want to work for themselves and start up their own cleaning company, but you were hoping they would go to university to get a degree, encourage them! You've got to respect their choice. Offer as much support and encouragement as possible and they will love you for it. If you don't respect what they want, and you try to coerce them into doing what you want them to do, they will resent you big time. They might even rebel against you.

It's true that people perform better when they are happy. I can say that from personal experience. Although I love what I do now, I didn't always love what I did. When I left school, I took all kinds of jobs, for the simple reason, I didn't know what I wanted to do. I quickly realised that I didn't like working for a boss. And I'm ashamed to admit, I wasn't the best employee, simply because I wasn't interested. But now that I work for myself, I work harder than I've ever worked in my life and I enjoy it. In fact, I don't look upon it as work, it's my passion. But I must also point out that my parents never coerced me into anything. They supported me in whatever I did, and have always encouraged me. But I think some of the blame must lie with the school system, because at school they don't teach you about working for yourself, they only teach you how to be an employee.

Looking back I can see that deep down, I always wanted to work for myself. I didn't recognise this consciously, but my subconscious did. As I was unknowingly suppressing this subconscious desire to be my own boss, I carried around much resentment without really knowing why. Then after several years, I had an opportunity to start my own business and my whole attitude changed virtually overnight. I developed enthusiasm, almost instantly, where I had none before. Suddenly I had a purpose. Instead of time dragging and constantly looking at the clock, time would fly. I would often say to myself "Is that the time already?" Because of my new-found enthusiasm, sleep seemed to get in the way, because I was looking forward to each day. Instead of dreading getting up in the morning, I was eager to get up and get started. Why do I tell you these things? So that you don't suppress your own children's desires by trying to make their career choices for them. I'll guarantee you that even if what they want to do seems trivial and unimportant to you, they will perform 100 percent better if you allow them the freedom to do it, than they would have, if you coerced them into doing something they didn't really want to do.

If you are the one looking to make a career choice and you are not quite sure what to do, consider asking yourself these questions first: (please note, there are no right or wrong answers)

DO YOU WANT TO WORK FOR YOURSELF OR SOMEONE ELSE?

I would say that this is the most important question of all, and is the one that should be asked before all the rest. Perhaps you want to work for someone else first, to gain some experience, and then branch out on your own. But this is not always necessary. Some businesses cost a lot of money to start up, whereas some businesses, such as cleaning business and MLM businesses can be started up for next to nothing, and with virtually no risk. It depends what type of business you want to do. Do you like taking orders from other people, or do you resent being told what to do? If you resent being told what to do, this is a strong indicator that you will most likely be happiest working for yourself.

DO YOU WANT TO WORK ON YOUR OWN, OR BE PART OF A TEAM?

Do you get on well with people? Or do you prefer your own company? If you prefer your own company you will still have to deal with people, but it doesn't mean you have to work with them. For example, a taxi driver is his own boss, but he still has to interact with people. Whereas if you join the army, you will be part of a team. Sometimes this can involve trial and error if you aren't sure. You might have to take a job in order to find out. That's exactly what happened to me, and it left me in no doubt.

DO YOU WANT TO BE INDOORS OR OUTDOORS?

There are plusses and minuses for each. Some people like to work indoors, but they won't get to enjoy the scorching heat on a hot summer's day, when everyone else is outdoors. People who work outdoors may get to enjoy the hot summer weather, but they will also have to put up with freezing cold weather in the winter. If you choose to work outside, you need to take the good with the bad, when it comes to the weather. In an office, it might be more comfortable, but you might also find yourself catching every bug during winter, whereas outside you may find that you are healthier, as the fresh air helps to kill of bugs etc.

DO YOU PREFER LOGIC OVER CREATIVITY?

The left part of our brain deals with logic, whereas the right side deals with creativity. For example someone who constantly deals with facts and figures, such as an accountant, is using logic the vast majority of the time. Whereas a musician, writer, artist or inventor is using the creative part of their brain most of the time. Which appeals to you the most? Not that there is a right or wrong answer, only different. But it has been proven that people who use the creative side of their brain, normally live longer than people who use mainly the left side of their brains. But, above all, remember to follow your heart. That is the bottom line.

TAKE ACTION

Let me ask you a question. If there are three frogs sitting on a log and two of them decide to jump into the water, how many does that leave? If you answered "one" you're wrong. Actually there are still three frogs left. The reason is that the two frogs only decided to jump in, they didn't back it up with action. You might think that sounds corny, but how many of us make decisions in our daily lives, but never actually do anything about it? I'm guilty of doing it myself, although I've made a decision to improve.

How many times have you heard people say they're going to do this or going to do that, only to find that it was a whole load of empty promises? Then you begin to doubt any further promises they make. Slowly but surely, they begin to lose credibility, until it gets to a point where everything they say, you take with a pinch of salt. Making a promise or commitment is one thing, but taking action is another. If you make a promise or commit to do something, make sure you follow through. Otherwise, don't make the commitment in the first place. Its far better to say you can't do it, and risk disappointing them, than to make the commitment and let them down. Because then you have compromised your integrity. Integrity is essential, if you want to be successful.

Some people, who break their commitments, make excuses such as "I didn't have the time" or "I forgot", but usually it is a case of priorities rather than time. All of us have a set of priorities. We all know, subconsciously, what is most important to us. So if we commit to something and break it, it is usually because it was too low down on our priority list to give it any attention. Even when we make the initial commitment, we often know, right there and then, if we are going to do it or not. Our inner voice is ticking away at a subconscious level, often without us knowing. Yet we might still make the commitment because we don't want to cause offence. Let me tell you, people will respect you far more, if you tell them up front that you can't make it. They will dislike you far more, if you make the commitment and then give them the run-around, and end up breaking the commitment.

THE QUALITY OF YOUR LIFE DEPENDS ON THE QUALITY OF YOUR DECISIONS

Our whole lives are made up of decisions. Each and every day, we make hundreds of decisions. Many people think that where they are in life right now, has something to do with 'chance' rather than choice. Often, they put it down to good luck or bad luck, and think that life is a matter of fate. But the truth is we have created our own circumstances and we are responsible for where we are right now.

Think about all the decisions a person might make in a day. Consider the case of Mike; He gets up in the morning- he has already decided what time the alarm will be set, the night before. He decides to lie in bed a further five minutes after the alarm goes off. He decides what to wear. He decides to have cereal instead of toast for breakfast. He decides to look at the clock to see what time it is. He decides to clean the kitchen when he comes home from work because he hasn't got time just now. He decides to walk to work instead of taking the car. He decides to take his i-pod with him. He decides to stop at a shop on the way there. He decides to check his mobile phone for text messages. He decides to wave to someone on the other side of the road. I won't bore you with any more, such trivial decisions, but you get the point don't you?

These decisions seem, and probably are quite trivial. But other decisions we make, have far reaching, and sometimes life-changing consequences. Often, decisions which seem unimportant at the time, can often have a major impact on the quality of our lives in the long term. For example, a person decides to have a fry-up for breakfast instead of cereal. No big deal. At least, not just now. But it becomes a daily habit and it continues for years. After a while, they put on weight and their health starts to suffer. Was it just coincidence that their health started to suffer? Not really. It was the result of daily decisions they made for years and years.

A person might decide to buy newspapers and magazines every day. There doesn't seem to be anything wrong with that. After all, everybody else does it! They also listen to the news every day and hear about all the terrible things happening in the world. As a result, they start thinking negatively and start to worry. They talk about these things in daily conversation, which reinforces it in their subconscious mind. This creates further negative emotions and they become pessimistic. One day, they realise they are not very happy and the world seems like a terrible place to be. Is it just coincidence that their attitude has been affected? Not really. It is a result of what they have allowed to go into their mind and what they have focused on. It has nothing to do with coincidence. It is a choice.

A person might choose to work for a boss, rather than own their own business. Deep down, they would really prefer to have their own business, but because of fear, they decide to work for a boss. They are afraid that if they work for themselves they might not always have enough work to provide them with a constant stream of income. (Making decisions based on fear, instead of faith) They allow the negative emotion of fear to steal their dream. As a result, they are not truly happy. And you never will be truly happy, as long as you allow fear, or any negative emotions to make your decisions for you. They complain about the pay and the boss, and they regard people who own their own businesses as 'lucky'. They think life is the pits and they hate getting up in the morning. But is it really a case of other people being lucky and them being unlucky? Not at all. It has everything to do with the decisions they made. They made a decision based on fear, and their fear has made them miserable. But neither are the other people who own their own businesses lucky. It was also a matter of choice for them too. They based their choice on courage, hope and probably faith too. They thought about how to succeed, rather than how to fail, and they took action. Different decisions, different results! Different level of happiness!

A person we shall call Joe, is fed up being shy and introverted, so he decides to develop a positive mental attitude and start taking an interest in other people. As a result, he becomes a chatty person. On the way to work, he walks along the road, smiling and saying good morning to people he doesn't even know. He feels good, and it also brightens up the other person's day. It is a classic win-win situation. When he's on public transport, he strikes up conversations with people he might not normally talk to. He asks them questions about themselves, such as where they work and where they come from. Occasionally, this sometimes leads to useful contacts. He also continually looks for things to compliment in people. For example, if the secretary has a new hairstyle he tells her how good it looks. Or if someone has a new car, or a new suit he likes, he lets them know.

One of the people Joe struck up a conversation with, has offered him an opportunity to massively increase his income, and own his own part time business. Joe is happier now than he has ever been in his life. He realises that the quality of your life depends on the quality of your relationships.

Is it just coincidence that Joe is happier, and has seemed to get the breaks? Is it just coincidence that people like Joe and bend over backwards to help him. Not at all. All of this is a result of the choices Joe has made, changing his habits and talking to people he might not normally talk to. Indirectly, Joe has actually made his own 'breaks' by the seeds he has sown. Now he is reaping the harvest. Nothing to do with chance, but everything to do with making decisions. Had he not made these decisions, he would probably still be in the same old rut.

You cannot avoid making decisions. If you are faced with a tough decision and you put off making that decision, that itself is a decision. To say that you don't want to choose is itself a choice. You had to choose to say that. If you procrastinate, you had to decide to procrastinate. But remember that success is also a choice. Success or failure are both choices. So how do you choose success? The same way you choose failure, by your daily decisions and habits. You don't choose it directly, you choose it indirectly by the choices you make each day. It's all the daily decisions, put together that lead to success (or failure). It's what you decide to do every day that will determine where you end up in life. One person might decide to let criticism or disappointment stop them while another decides to persist and keep taking action. Its your decision. Have you decided to take on board what I have said? Have you decided to change your habits? Have you decided to take action and do something with your life? Only you can decide. No one can decide for you.

WORRY ABOUT IT OR DEAL WITH IT, YOU CAN'T DO BOTH

When you are faced with circumstances which cause anxiety or fear, you have a choice; you can either worry about it, or you can deal with it. You **can't** do both. Taking action (dealing with it) is constructive, and is the only way you can successfully do something about it. But worrying about it is destructive and accomplishes nothing. If you are dealing with it, then you are not worrying. But if you are worrying, then you are not dealing with it. When you take action, you begin to reduce fear, because you are too busy taking action to be worrying. You cannot be thinking two different things at the same time. While you are dealing with it, you are so busy concentrating on the task at hand, that there is no place for worry. But when you are worrying, you are usually doing nothing, at that particular moment.

Fear is mostly imaginative, and when you take action, you reduce the size of the obstacle in your own mind. Taking action causes certain changes to take place in your brain and gives you a feeling of confidence, which gradually replaces fear. The more action you take, the smaller the fear becomes, and the greater your confidence becomes. The flip-side is that taking no action, and sitting at home worrying about something actually does the opposite. Fear increases and you actually lose confidence.

If you give into your fear, you have now allowed the fear to control you. Avoiding something because of fear, increases fear. Since you haven't faced it, you don't know the facts. And when you don't know the facts, your imagination takes over. When your imagination takes over, it has a tendency to enlarge things. The more time that passes by, the bigger they get in your own mind. This is how giving into fear and worry have a multiplying effect, and can paralyse us.

Conversely, facing your fears also has a multiplying effect, in a positive sense. If you make a habit of facing your fears, your self confidence increases, and your self image sky-rockets. You also develop belief in yourself. When you face even the smallest of fears, this makes it easier to face other fears, and becomes a stepping stone to building self confidence and belief in yourself. Your inner voice goes something like this: "I know that I faced my fear the last time, therefore I believe I can also conquer this other fear". Your self image changes each time you face your fear, and although you may not realise it, you are a different person, subconsciously.

Let's suppose you have two main fears. Fear 'A' and fear 'B'. They can be about anything you choose, but this is just an example. You face fear 'A' and you gain some self confidence. You are now a different person (in terms of self image) than you were before you faced the fear. You have grown mentally, even if only slightly. So, when you face your next fear (fear 'B') you are facing it with a different perspective and with a different level of confidence than when you faced fear 'A'. As you face fear 'B' with a new level of confidence, you find it easier to face your next fear (fear 'C'). And on it goes. As long as you are facing your fears, it becomes an upward spiral of self confidence, rather than a downward spiral of fear. But it is a choice nevertheless. Some people choose to face their fears but other people avoid what they fear.

On the other side of fear is freedom, but on this side of fear is bondage and misery. But the good news is, you don't have to be on this side. Even if you are on this side just now, you can smash through it, by facing your fear and taking action. Then you will see fear for what it really is ; an emotion cultivated by our own imagination, designed to keep us enslaved and in bondage. Although it appears real, it can be destroyed by taking action.

FOLLOW YOUR HUNCHES

It often pays to follow your hunches. There is much debate over where a hunch comes from. Some people call it a sixth sense, some say it is the workings of your subconscious mind, others say hunches come directly from God. No-one can say for sure, but my personal view is that if something is for the highest good, is beneficial and also opposes evil, then it could well be from God.

One of the most decisive naval battles in history was won, following a hunch by Commander Wade McClusky during the Battle of Midway in early June 1942. Admiral Chester Nimitz later described this as the most important decision of the battle. Six months after the attack on Pearl Harbour the Japanese planned an attack on Midway atoll, which is a small island, half way between the US state of Hawaii and the coast of Japan.

The Japanese, having failed to destroy the American air-craft carriers at Pearl Harbour, wanted to lure the American fleet into the open sea and destroy it once and for all.

American intelligence had broken the Japanese codes, and they (the Japanese) didn't know it. When the Japanese attacked Midway, the Americans had fortified the island and were waiting. The American fighters and bombers were in the air, and out of the way. Unfortunately for the Japanese, the initial attack inflicted heavy damage but failed. A second attack was needed. The Japanese reserve aircraft, on board their aircraft carriers were presently armed with anti-shipping torpedoes, in case American ships were sighted. So Admiral Chuichi Nagumo ordered that his aircraft be taken below and torpedoes replaced by general purpose bombs, for attacking Midway. But part way through this process he got word that a sizeable American fleet had been sighted to the east. Nagumo was now in a dilemma; half his strike force were fitted with bombs, the other half with torpedoes. Should he concentrate on Midway or the American ships? He decided to wait until the first wave of his aircraft returned from attacking Midway, and then fit all aircraft with torpedoes.

Meanwhile the Americans had launched 150 more aircraft

from the carriers Enterprise and Hornet, to search for the Japanese carriers. The Americans knew that the Japanese would soon be landing aircraft after the attack on Midway. But in the vast expanse of the deep blue Pacific Ocean, the Americans had difficulty finding their enemy. Lieutenant Commander McClusky, leading 33 dive bombers, scanned the Pacific, north east of Midway. But where he expected to find the enemy, he found nothing. His planes would soon have to turn back for lack of fuel. But McClusky had a hunch. He decided to continue his search further to the west.

A few minutes later McClusky spotted the wake of an enemy destroyer and followed it. They had found the Japanese carriers. McClusky was also joined by another 17 divebombers from USS Yorktown. These pilots were to make probably the most decisive naval air strike in history. For the Japanese, this could not have happened at a worse moment. They had abandoned all safety procedures, as they hurriedly switched their aircraft from bombs to torpedoes. Fuel hoses were everywhere, as planes were being refuelled and ammunition was stacked all over the decks. The decks of the Japanese carriers were crammed with nearly 100 aircraft, as they prepared for their own strike against the US carriers. Loaded with explosives and high octane fuel, the slightest spark would have turned them into a fireball.

Just as the Japanese carriers were turning into the wind to launch their aircraft, the American dive bombers appeared overhead. The first bombs hit three Japanese carriers, 'Akagi', 'Kaga' and 'Soryu' and turned them into floating infernos. Three out of four of Japans largest aircraft carriers, which launched the attack on Pearl Harbour six months earlier, were blazing from end to end. Within minutes, most of Japans first air fleet had been wiped out.

The fourth Japanese carrier 'Hiryu' had somehow become separated from the other three and was saved. It managed to launch a desperate counter attack against the USS Yorktown. The Yorktown fought hard for survival against the Japanese bombers, but in vain. It took several hits and was later sunk by a Japanese submarine. A few hours later, aircraft were launched from carriers 'Hornet' and 'Enterprise'. Their mission? To attack the carrier 'Hiryu'. Once again, the Japanese were taken by surprise, as their aircraft were on deck preparing for a strike against the US carriers. Four direct hits turned her into a blazing fireball.

The Battle of Midway was a turning point in the Pacific war, and was a defeat from which Japan would never recover. On June 6 1942 Admiral Yamamoto gave the order for a general withdrawal. The Japanese had lost 4 of their largest aircraft carriers, a heavy cruiser, 322 aircraft and about 500 men. The United States had lost 1 aircraft carrier, 137 aircraft and about 307 men.

Recently, the Yorktown has been located at the bottom of the ocean, with her guns still pointed at the sky, a war grave and a tribute to the brave men who fought for our freedom. Had McClusky not acted on his hunch, who knows what might have happened?

THE ULTIMATE COUNSELLOR

I can only speak from my own experience and what has helped me, but God has helped me in ways I could never have imagined possible. Only God could have gotten me out of the rut I was in. Looking back at my life, God has often helped me the most when I deserved it the least. But God is faithful, even when we're not. "If we are faithless, he will remain faithful, for he cannot disown himself" (2 Tim 2: 13)

When we have problems and we don't know what to do, the best thing we can do is take it to the Lord. This doesn't mean that we will be spared from pain or hardship, but "We know that in all things God works for the good of those who love him, who have been called according to his purpose" (Rom 8: 28) It may be painful in the short term, but ultimately we know that things will work out for our highest good in the long term.

Sometimes the answer we get from God is not always immediate and we don't always understand why we get that particular answer. But we are told "I will instruct you and teach you in the way you should go; I will counsel you and watch over you" (Psalm 32 : 8) The counsel we get could come in any shape or form. It could come from a person, or it might come from a book or a seminar. It might come in the form of a vivid thought or an idea. It could come from an infinite number of ways, and often unexpected ways, which to an unbeliever, might seem like 'coincidence'. But God will answer us. We are told in the book of Job "For God does speak - now one way, now another - though man may not perceive it" (Job 33: 14)

The Holy Spirit is the best Counsellor we will ever have and is with us forever. Shortly before Jesus was to be crucified, his disciples were dismayed because they knew he was leaving them. But Jesus comforted them by saying "And I will ask the Father, and he will give you another Counsellor to be with you forever--the Spirit of truth. The world cannot accept him, because it neither sees him nor knows him. But you know him, for he lives with you and will be in you" (John 14 : 15-17)

CHAPTER 8

YOUR DREAMS

Do you know who the biggest dreamers are? Do you know who has the most self belief? The answer is children. A lot of children would put us adults to shame with their lofty ambitions for the future. A lot of them would put us to shame with their self confidence and how big they think. Children don't know any limits and they probably haven't lost their self confidence yet because they are still too young. To them, the sky's the limit, because they've not yet learned to think negatively. But wait until adulthood and it's a different story. What happened? Life happened. It got knocked out of them. Sad but true.

If you were to question a group of children about what they wanted to achieve in life, you would probably get a far more positive response than you would if you were to ask a group of adults. You would hear all kinds of ambitious responses, which to many adult ears would sound far-fetched or unrealistic. You might hear things like "I want to be a fighter pilot" or "I want to be an actor, or a musician" or "I want to be a spaceman" Sadly, many dreams are quashed right there and then, as they are told "You can't do that" or to "be realistic" And what happens to their inner voice? Eventually when they are told repeatedly that they can't do this or can't do that, their inner voice starts to change. It goes from believing they can, to believing they can't. This doesn't mean that their dreams have disappeared, they simply get suppressed. They get buried deeper and deeper, under layers of negative self talk, until their dreams are eventually forgotten.

Later on in life, as they become adults, they can often be very cynical if they are presented with an opportunity to better themselves or become financially independent, because they have told themselves for such a long time to stop living in fantasy land and just settle for mediocrity. For the few who do dare to step out and go for their dreams, it can often take years of

177

re-programming their minds, to undo the damage that has been done by negative thinking. It can often take them equally as long to begin to believe in themselves, or to believe it is possible to achieve their dreams.

What do you want out of life? That's a very powerful question isn't it? But one we are very seldom asked, if ever! Amazingly, if you were to stop people at random, in the street and ask them what they wanted to achieve in life, the vast majority of them probably couldn't tell you. It's not that they don't want anything, it's just that we are not used to thinking that way. Society doesn't teach us to dream. Infact, it usually does the opposite and knocks our dreams out of us. People tell us our ideas won't work, they criticise and ridicule us. But society will only knock your dreams out of you if you allow it. It won't happen unless you allow it to happen. It is a choice that you make. Instead, you can if you want, choose to pursue your dreams, in spite of what society says.

Many people had their dreams knocked out of them when they were younger, by well meaning but ignorant adults. These adults were often parents or school teachers, who said "Stop dreaming and grow up! Instead, tell me what kind of job you want" By the time children reach adulthood, they may well have talked themselves out of their own dreams because of a lack of belief in themselves, and learned to settle for a life of mediocrity. For example, how often do you hear your friends or colleagues talking about pursuing their dreams, or becoming financially independent? How often, at school did you hear your teachers talking about achieving dreams or becoming wealthy? Probably never. Unfortunately, the whole of society is geared to keep us average. At school, we are only taught how to get a job, which means that at a very young age, we are already having our thinking moulded and shaped to go in a particular direction. If you want to achieve your dreams, it's going to be a continual uphill battle against the forces of mediocrity that are trying to pull you down and stop you from succeeding.

Society might tempt us to go for a job with a fancy title and benefits, but we can never be financially free working for a boss. Because no matter how much money we make, we will never have the time to go with it. We will always be in a position where we are being controlled. We might have to work with negative people who also try and pull us down, by destroying our positive attitude. And in this day and age, there is no such thing as job security.

Society also tries to steal our dreams by keeping us broke, and encouraging us to get into debt. Almost every week, we get things through the door saying "Buy Now, Pay Later!" which unfortunately lures many people into the trap of paying 'killer interest'. This destroys their finances and can also destroy their happiness. Buying things on credit is very short term thinking, which very often leads to serious financial difficulties later on.

Getting into debt is not the way to wealth; it is the way to poverty, unless it is debt which will improve your financial situation. Debt such as taking out a mortgage on a rental property, where the rental income is greater than your expenditures is classed as 'good debt'. For example, if I purchase a rental property and the rental income is £500 a month, but my total expenditures, including the mortgage is only £400 a month, then that is good debt because I'm £100 in front, and I also own the property, which goes up in value. But any kind of debt which provides no income or where the income is less than the expenditure is bad debt. There again, it is your choice. No-one is forcing you to do go into debt, but you could, if you wish, say to yourself "Unless I can buy something cash, I will do without" which is far more sensible. Then you are on the track to wealth. This requires discipline, and may be a bit painful at first, but eventually the long term benefits will start to pay off.

Negative people also try to pull us down by criticising us and telling us that our ideas won't work. If we listen to them, we may well be in danger of abandoning our dreams, and settling for a life of mediocrity. The only way to stand up to negative people is by constant, positive, daily reinforcement of what you allow into your mind. The other danger is the media; things such as newspapers, and negative TV programmes, all cause negative emotions which destroy our happiness and take us further away from our dreams. Society will not drag you down if you make positive choices. Only if you make negative choices, will it drag you down. If you want to achieve your dreams, you need to be different. You can't be doing what everybody else is doing and expect to get different results. It doesn't work that way. If you want different results from everyone else then you're going to have to do different things from everyone else. You're going to have to sacrifice. You're going to have to discipline yourself. You're going to have to develop some new habits and give up some old habits. You're going to have to put the effort in. You're going to have to become something of a non-conformist.

Let me ask you a question, what do you think would be most beneficial for your body, in order to make it perform at its best? Filling it with vitamins, fibre, carbohydrates and proteins, or filling it with smoke, alcohol and grease? Not a hard question to answer is it? Yet many people fill their bodies with smoke, alcohol and grease every day, and they wonder why their health isn't as good as it should be. In the same way, you can't expect to achieve your dreams, and your mind to operate effectively by filling it with all kinds of negative junk. When you fill your mind with radio, newspapers and TV, it is the equivalent to filling your body with alcohol smoke and grease. It won't function very well and it will stand between you and your dreams.

When you start to pursue your dreams, people might even think of you as some sort of odd ball. But that's okay! That simply means you're on the road to success! Take a look back at the history books and see what people thought of dreamers then. What did people think of the Wright brothers? No-one had ever flown before, but they were going to fly this thing through the air! Yeah, sure! But they did it! And look at how much aviation has advanced since then! No man had ever been to another planet before, because it was literally inconceivable, yet Neil Armstrong made history in 1969 by being the first person to walk on the moon. His famous words were "One small step for man, but one giant leap for mankind" and it certainly was!

Walt Disney knew that success meant going against what the masses thought. He had a rule, that when he had an idea, he would bring ten of his advisors into a room and explain the idea to them. If at least nine of them didn't think he was crazy, he would discard the idea. And we all know how successful Walt Disney was! So don't worry if people ridicule you or tell you that you're crazy, or that your ideas won't work. That stuff is to be expected, so you might as well get used to it right now! That's if you want to achieve your dreams, of course. If you're experiencing some of that, congratulations!! Join the club! It means you're doing something worthwhile. You can now join the ranks of the achievers who want to do something worthwhile with their lives.

People who achieve greatly in life are usually people with vision. That means they can see something in their imagination that other people cannot see. I'm not talking about anything mystical. I simply mean that being a dreamer means being able to see it in your mind's eye, and to believe it is possible, even although it might seem like a million miles away just now. You need to be able to do this in the face of adversity and when people all around you are telling you that it's a silly idea. You need to be able to do this when faced with disappointment and when you feel like giving up. In short, it's your dream that will keep you going.

Great achievers are often very 'unrealistic' in their thinking. They believe possible, what other people believe is impossible. They think 'outside the box' and have different habits from the masses. They are willing to persist and do whatever it takes to get there. They don't say "I'll give it a try", they say "I'll do whatever it takes"-- end of story! They learn to handle criticism, rejection and ridicule because they know that means they are on the right track. Yes, they also have fears like you and I, but they learn to face their fears and they take action.

SETTING GOALS AND BUILDING THE DREAM

When I first heard about dream building or having some sort of dream-board, I thought it was kind of crazy. I thought it was sort of childish or fairytale-ish to cut out pictures of your dreams and put them together on a board. But after doing it, I now realise how important it is. Not only does it work, but it also fun to dream! Try it! What could be more fun than spending time putting together a collection of your life ambitions, or places you want to visit and putting them together on a dream board? It certainly helps to put the enthusiasm back into your life and motivates you. It also provides very definite and specific targets for your subconscious to aim at. Why not get rid of that negative poster or negative fridge magnet and have a picture of your dream instead? Maybe it's a dream home, maybe it's a certain holiday resort, or maybe it's paying off the mortgage. Maybe it's a goal to earn more money. For example, if you earn £50,000 a year and you want to earn £100,000 a year, you might put a sign on your fridge which says "I am now earning £100,000 every year" It doesn't necessarily have to be on the fridge, just as long as you can see it every day. But whatever it is, having pictures of your dreams will be far more beneficial than having some negative fridge magnet or some poster on your wall. But it has to be somewhere it can be seen daily. Remember, out of sight means out of mind.

If for example, you need to make an extra £1000 a month in order to buy to buy a new car, then why not write down the exact amount you need to be making, and put it next to the picture of the car? For example, if you are making £2000 a month just now and you need to be making £3000 a month to buy a new car, why not write down "I am now making £3000 a month" and put it next to the picture of your dream car? You might be surprised at what happens.

Most people are unaware that simply cutting out a picture or writing something down has a huge impact on your subconscious mind. The more emotional impact your dream has on you, the more likely you are to achieve it. Without even realising it, your subconscious will start to take you in that direction. How you think consciously, and the decisions you make, will also change. Therefore, your actions will change. You might be motivated to go the extra mile, or make a few extra contacts, all because you now have a dream which you can see with your eyes. You will attract people and opportunities to help bring it about. Let me tell you, there is tremendous power in the dream. The dream energises you and motivates you. It gives you a reason to keep going when you feel like quitting, but you have to put the effort in. A dream without work is mere fantasy, but work without a dream is drudgery. Sadly, many people go to work every day without a dream. Therefore it comes as no surprise that many people look upon their jobs as drudgery. It reminds me of the hamster in the wheel. It goes round and round, with no real reward at the end of it. You could forgive it for thinking "This scenery looks kind of familiar, I'm putting in a lot of effort and getting nowhere fast" Although you might feel like that about your job, don't lose heart because you have far more hope than a hamster. You can start a part time business in your spare time and get involved in a personal development programme, a hamster can't.

I believe there is a dream inside everybody; they just haven't found it yet. In my opinion many people don't bother to dream because they don't believe it is possible, and they don't want to get disappointed. They think it is better not to dream, than to get your hopes up and risk disappointment. Let me tell you, that is a failure attitude that you need to get rid of right this second! Not only is it a huge mistake, but it is also one of the biggest reasons people never achieve their dreams. For something to be possible, you first have to believe it is possible, or you will sabotage your own success. The only person that will stop you from achieving your dreams is you! Sometimes we are our own biggest obstacles!

Don't think that just because you work for a boss, or hate your job, that you can't achieve your dreams. Of course you can! But it will almost definitely mean starting some other kind of venture in your spare time. If you are working at a job you hate, and you can't see how on earth your dreams can be possible, let me tell you something; I was once in the exact same position as you. And if I can get out of it, so can you. My advice to you is this : the best thing you can do right now is to get involved in personal development, while still working your job, even if you can't see an opportunity at the moment. Don't wait until an opportunity arises first, do it NOW! Go to your local bookstore today, or at the very latest, tomorrow and buy a book from the self-help section, and make a habit of buying a new book every month. That's an excellent start! It's amazing how the more positive you become, the more you seem to attract opportunities. No matter what your circumstances, or how hopeless things seem, let me tell you, YOUR DREAM IS POSSIBLE! You just need to work out what you really want, write it down or have pictures of it. Then you need to develop a plan of action, and find an opportunity that will allow you to make enough extra money to achieve your dream. And last but not least, you need to be prepared to work! Work! Work! Remember, there's no such thing as a free lunch. Yes, your dream is possible, but you're not going to achieve it by simply cutting out pictures and doing nothing. You need to do something. If you're not sure what you can do to make extra money, why not ask God for an opportunity? Turn your problems over to Him. If you're willing to do your part (put the effort in) God will surely do His part and provide you with the opportunity. "Until now you have not asked for anything in my name, ask and you will receive and your joy will be complete" (John 16: 24)

If you don't believe you can achieve your dreams, realise that the fault lies in your own belief system, not in circumstances. The Bible says "All things are possible for him who believes" (Mark 9: 23) Yes, I admit, there are times when we all get disappointed, but you don't give up just because someone or something disappoints you! You keep going! Therefore, if you want to achieve your dreams, it's time to start believing it's possible, because it is! Once again, your own thinking will determine whether you succeed or fail. If you believe you can, you can, but if you believe you can't, you're right too!

The dream also releases energy that you never knew you had. It causes you to get up out of your chair and take action. When you have a dream, you don't mind going out in the evening, in freezing cold weather to share the presentation with someone, because you know that you're present situation is only temporary. You remind yourself why you're doing it. It may be because you're going to be on the beaches of the world, soaking up the scorching hot sunshine, while everyone else is back home complaining about the weather, and having to get up for work. You visualise yourself in your holiday apartment, looking out from the veranda, where you can see people swimming in the deep blue sea. You see the beauty of the hills on the horizon. The temperature is 30 Celsius, and you visualise yourself going down to the pool where everyone is out sunbathing and having cold drinks. You look at your watch and remind yourself that at this particular time back home, everyone else will be battling rush hour traffic, trying to get to work. But the reason you are able to do this is because you didn't give up on your dream! Many of the people back home, battling the rush hour traffic, were the naysayers who told you, you couldn't do it. You're sure glad you didn't listen to them!

While not all of my dreams have come true (yet), many of them have. Some I have had to reset because I achieved them. For example, I remember setting a goal to own my first rental property. I cut out a picture of a house I liked and stuck it on my dream board, and put the words "For Rent" next to it. After a few years, it eventually happened. But it didn't just magically happen, because at the time I set the goal, there was no way on earth that I could have afforded a second home. But you don't wait until you have the money before you set the goal, you set the goal, even when it looks 'impossible', and then your subconscious will start to take you in that direction. Gradually my financial situation began to improve, certain events took place and situations transpired, which made owning a second home possible. But it did not work out in the way I had envisioned it. Logically, I could not see a way. But remember, faith has no logic. The opportunity came about in a very unexpected way. I won't go into all the details but I will just say that I believe it was the work of Almighty God. I believe He provided the opportunity. There's no way I could have done it on my own.

Sure I had to put the effort in, I had to look at the property market and give up my time to view houses, but it was worth it! Had I never set the goal, I probably wouldn't have taken those steps. As soon as I achieved that goal, I immediately reset the goal to own two rental properties, because the most dangerous thing you can do is hit a goal without having another one in place. If you hit a goal without having another one in place, you're at the point of sliding backwards. We always need to be striving towards something. There always has to be 'another goal'. After all, that's what makes life exciting! But the important thing is what YOU want to achieve. I am merely using mine as an example.

What I did, was get myself a picture frame which was about two feet long by about a foot, and used it for a collection of all my goals and dreams. I then put it somewhere I could see it every day. I had a picture of rental property I wanted to own, there were holiday resorts and historic islands I wanted to visit. I had a goal for earning two or three times what I was actually earning. Some people might think that is thinking too small, but every time my financial situation improved and I started to get close to my goal, I would raise the goal even higher, so that my financial situation continued to keep improving too. It works and continues to work!

I also had a goal which said "I am now a bestselling author" Incidentally, when I set this goal, I didn't even have a publisher. I had written my very first manuscript, which took a year to write and I wasn't even assured of getting a publisher at all. I had written it in total faith that I would get a publisher, but I was getting rejection after rejection. It certainly was discouraging but I didn't give up hope, and neither was I going to. But while all this was going on, the goal was still in place, because you always set a goal according to what you want, even if your present circumstances look the total opposite.

Yes, I am an author, I have achieved that part, but am I a bestselling author? At this precise moment it is too early to say. It depends on whether people like yourself buy my book or not (only joking!) But whether it becomes a bestseller or not will not deter me from setting the goal, because you need to dream big. My prayer is that my books will help change as many peoples lives as possible. Therefore, I will set the goal, but the rest is outside my control. Even if my book didn't become a bestseller, I would still rather have set the goal and failed, than failed to set the goal and succeeded. Why think small? Why limit yourself? If you think small and set small goals, you will get small results.

How many people do you know who have written down

their dreams? How many people do you know who have actually achieved them? Probably the same amount. Interesting isn't it? A coincidence? I don't think so. A study at Harvard University revealed that of all the students, only 10 percent had goals. Of the 10 percent, only 3 percent had written them down, the other 7 percent knew what they wanted, but didn't bother to write them down.

Interestingly, the 3 percent group was traced many years later and it was discovered that the 3 percent group had not only achieved their goals, but they had more wealth than the 97 percent combined, of equal intelligence! Is it important to write your dreams and goals down? You bet it is!

WHAT EXACTLY DO YOU WANT?

What you would really like to do, if time and money were unlimited? Do any of the following appeal to you? You might even want to come up with some of your own ideas.

- EARLY RETIREMENT
- PAY OFF MORTGAGE
- START YOUR OWN BUSINESS (BE YOUR OWN BOSS)
- A NEW CAR
- PERSONAL DEVELOPMENT
- GIVE MONEY TO CHARITY
- GIVE YOUR TIME WORKING FOR CHARITABLE CAUSES
- A BIGGER HOME IN THE COUNTRYSIDE
- A HOME IN THE TOWN
- A HOUSE WITH NO NEIGHBOURS
- A HOLIDAY HOME ABROAD
- SPEND MORE TIME WITH YOUR FAMILY AND LOVED ONES
- HILLWALKING
- CANOEING

- TAKE UP ART
- LEARN A NEW SUBJECT
- NEW CLOTHES
- BUY YOUR OWN PERSONAL BOAT
- GO TO A BEAUTY SPA
- RENTAL PROPERTY
- TAKE FLYING LESSONS
- OWN YOUR OWN PLANE OR HELICOPTER
- DINING OUT WITH YOUR SPOUSE MORE OFTEN
- MORE TIME TO KEEP FIT AND PLAY SPORT
- FINANCIAL FREEDOM

Once you have decided what you want to achieve, the more real you can make it to your subconscious mind, the better. That's why pictures are so powerful. If there is a certain car you want, go down to the dealership and test drive it. Sit in it and make it real to your subconscious. Decide what colour you want. Get a picture of it and put it on your dream board.

A top businessman in the MLM business was once asked what were the top ten most important parts of the business, and he replied "Number one is the dream, number two is the dream, number three is the dream, number four is the dream, number five is the dream, number six is the dream, number seven is the dream, number eight is the dream, number nine is the dream and number ten is the dream. So dream big and keep your dream in front of you!"

Being as specific as possible, is also vitally important. For example, rather than just say "I want to travel" which is too vague, you might say something like "I would love to go to Hawaii, or "I would love to see the Eiffel Tower" or "I would love to visit the Great Wall of China" But just for the sake of an example, let's say that you want to own and live in a big mansion in the country. If you can get a picture of it, that's great, but if you can go and visit it, that's even better! Nothing is more real, than experiencing the real thing! This is ultimate dream building! If there's a particular car you want, you may be able to go down to the dealership and see it. But you don't just visit it once and say "That's it, I've done it!" You do it regularly, maybe once a week or maybe once a month. Do it regularly, and never get so bogged down in the work that you lose sight of your dream. Never forget 'why' you are doing something. After all, it's the 'why' that gives you the energy to do the 'how'.

Often the best time to go dream building is when you're having a tough time. Perhaps you're faced with disappointment and you feel like giving up. That's exactly when you need to focus on your dream! If you like boats, then take a trip down to the harbour. That may be the time to get in the car and go visit your dream home. If it's not possible to visit it, then take some time out to visualise your dream. Look at pictures of it. Do some dream building. Then, in your mind's eye, imagine what it will really be like to be in the house right now, knowing that you own it. But here's where you need to be specific, because you cannot present a clear cut definite image to your subconscious, if it is too vague. It has to be specific, if it is to make an impression.

Let me just say that the more of the five senses you involve in this process, the more real it will be to your subconscious mind, because your subconscious cannot tell the difference between a real experience and one vividly imagined, remember? For example, how many rooms does it have? Does it have modern windows or old fashioned windows? What colour is the stonework? Is it surrounded by trees? How high are the trees? Are there trees on every side of the house? What kind of trees are they? How much land do you have surrounding the house? Is the grass well kept and maintained? Do you have a perimeter wall going all the way round your property? Do you have an intercom and CCTV at the gates? Do you have a name for your house? Do you have a long winding driveway about a quarter of a mile long, because the grounds are so big? Do you have slabs or chips? Do you have guard dogs? Do you have a coal fire? What kind of car(s) do you have in your driveway?

Is it night time or is it day time? If it is night time, what sounds do you hear? Do you hear an owl in the distance? Or is it really quiet, except for the slight hum of the motorway in the distance? If there is a slight breeze, do you hear the trees rustling in the wind? Maybe that's all you can hear! Or can you hear the chips under you feet, as you walk to your car? Is there a river nearby? Maybe you can faintly hear running water in the distance? You look up at the sky and it's a beautiful starry night and a clear sky. You can see more stars than normal because there is less pollution than in the town. Maybe you are walking to your car and the moonlight is lighting up the driveway. It looks so peaceful. What smells can you smell? Can you smell the freshly cut grass and the scent from the trees? Maybe you can smell freshly cut logs that you use for your coal fire?

What about inside the house? What do you use the rooms for? Do you have a room specifically for watching TV? Do you have a fitness room? Maybe you have a separate room for studying, where you can read, or use the computer, without being disturbed?

Do you have a games room, where you can play snooker, and table tennis? Do you have an indoor sauna and Jacuzzi? Do you have a swimming pool? Maybe you have a room specifically for guests, and you don't have to worry about playing your music too loud because you don't have any neighbours? Is the house completely paid for? If that's your goal, then put the words "Paid For" or "Debt Free" next to it, on your dream board.

Now that may interest you, or it may not. If not, that's fine, but you need to find out what 'you' want. That's what matters! Maybe your dream is to give your money or time to charity. Maybe you have a special charity that means a lot to you, such as cancer research or helping people in the third world to dig wells, build hospitals, and help them to get educated. Maybe you want to give money to people dying of starvation, or to blinded war veterans who fought for our freedom? Maybe you want to donate money to people who need lifesaving operations? Maybe you want to adopt a child in a foreign country? Maybe you want to adopt a lot of children? Maybe you want to donate money to provide Bibles for people who have never heard of Jesus? Maybe you can help to provide light in the darkness, and change someone's life? Maybe you will be the one who prevents someone from committing suicide? You might be the one who gives someone hope, or the will to carry on? You never know what difference one person can make! Maybe you want to write self help books, and give out free copies to people who have lost hope? There is no limit to what you can do, if you believe it is possible. You are only limited by your own imagination and your own thinking. What are you thinking right now?

Maybe your dream is to be able to go to a hot country whenever you want, for as long as you want, and with who you want? At the moment it's not possible because you can't get the time off work. Neither can you afford to go very often, because you have bills to pay. Therefore, maybe your dream is to have more time and more money, so that you can do these things? Maybe, making more money will get rid of some of the stress and financial worries? If your dream is to spend more time on the sun-kissed beaches of the world, imagine what it will be like. Visualise it. Imagine all the bleached white holiday apartments along the sea front. Imagine the hired mopeds whizzing back and forwards. Imagine the beach packed with holiday makers, and the deep blue sea. Imagine people swimming and playing on the boats. Imagine drinking a glass of ice-cold freshly squeezed orange juice because the temperature is so hot.

What do you hear? Do you hear the laughter on the beach and the noise of the waves? Do you hear the sound of the vehicles passing along the sea front? Maybe someone next to you is playing music? Maybe your friends are shouting on you? What about the sense of touch? What do you feel? Do you feel the burning hot sand under the soles of your feet? Do you feel the scorching heat from the sun beating down on your back? Imagine how therapeutic it feels to have the sun's rays on your body. What about the sense of smell? What do you smell? Do you smell the suntan lotion and the salt water from the sea? If there is a food stall nearby, do you smell the smell of hot dogs or hamburgers? All of these things make it more real to your subconscious, and increases your chances of achieving it, because it motivates you to go out and do the work.

DREAMING DOESN'T HURT, IT ALTERS YOU STATE
OF MIND

Did you notice something about how I phrased the questions in the above paragraphs? If you did, well done! You are ultra-observant! If not, don't worry about it. But out of all the questions I asked, in relation to the dream, I used the present tense. I didn't say, for example, "What 'will' you use the rooms for?" I said "What 'do' you use the rooms for?" There's a big difference because one indicates the future tense (not yet happened) and the other indicates present tense (you have already achieved it) Tense is extremely important when setting goals or talking about your dreams. As long as you are talking about something which is yet to happen, it will probably remain in the future. That's why you should always speak about something, as though it is a reality right now, even though it seems like a million miles away. Then you will start to attract it.

If you say to yourself "I will use the rooms for......" you are reinforcing to your subconscious that it is not a present reality. But if you say to yourself "I use the rooms for........" it indicates to your subconscious that it is a reality right now, which is exactly what you want. Even if it isn't a reality, do it anyway!

Before you get annoyed at me or start protesting, just bear with me, and let me explain the mental chemistry behind it. Occasionally, you might hear people saying that they don't want to dream because it's too painful. And I can understand that, because I felt the same way in the beginning. But at some point, you've got to step out and take a chance, or you never will achieve it. How can you possibly achieve something without focusing on it? You can't! Imagine the Wright Brothers saying "I don't want to dream about flying because it hurts too much" Yet they still hoped to fly! Or Neil Armstrong saying "I don't want to think about walking on the moon in case it doesn't come true, and I get disappointed" Of course he focused on it! He focused on it big time!

When you dream, you are presenting an idea (or goal) to

your subconscious, which it will then act upon. If you don't dream, then it has nothing to act upon. You actually change your state of mind when you dream. It mentally puts you in the frame of mind that it's already yours. That's if it's vivid enough. For example, if you wanted to own a Ferrari, and you made a point of sitting in one, or test driving one every week, that is very real to your subconscious mind. You start to get used to the feeling. And it is this feeling that is important. Remember that emotions play a big part in impressing something on your subconscious mind. The more emotion, the bigger an impression it will make. Another key to impressing something upon the subconscious is repetition. The more often you do it, the quicker the idea will be accepted by your subconscious mind. When you combine emotion with repetition, it is immensely powerful. That's why dream building is so powerful. That's also why it works!

BUT THE PICTURE DOESN'T MATCH!

Let's use the Ferrari as an example. Suppose your goal is to own a Ferrari, but you only have an old rust bucket just now because that is all you can afford. At this precise moment, your subconscious has an image of an old rust bucket, because that's where you're at, just now. But when you go and sit in a Ferrari, or test drive one on a regular basis, you are starting to create a new mental image. You are starting to create the image of owning a Ferrari. While this is exactly what you want to do, your subconscious also recognises that the pictures don't match up. What I mean is, your subconscious sees what your present situation is just now (having an old rust bucket) and it also begins to accept the new image (of a Ferrari) that you are presenting to it.

Your subconscious always wants to have equilibrium and balance, so it says to itself "I had better do something about this, to make the pictures match up" and it is forced to devise ways of attracting it (the Ferrari) Then there will be equilibrium and balance. The subconscious hates discord. That's why it also hates change, because change means upsetting the way that things have always been done. It means upsetting the picture your subconscious has of you. Therefore it is a battle to achieve your dreams. That's why it is also a battle to improve your self image, or create self confidence, especially if you've never been confident before, because you are giving your subconscious a conflicting image than it's been used to. Therefore, it will fight against it, to begin with, but through persistence and utilising the power of emotion and repetition, your subconscious will eventually accept whatever it is presented with. So don't give up, and keep dreaming! It may take some time, but you'll get there.

THINK BIG, EVEN WHEN YOUR FINANCES ARE SMALL

I remember speaking to someone who had seen the car of their dreams. It was a beautiful car and was just what they had always wanted. But there was only one problem; money! There was no way at this present moment they could afford it. So I advised them to get a picture of it and put it somewhere they could see it every day, but they refused. They said "What's the point? I can't afford it! Where am I going to get the money to buy a car like that?" In other words, they were going to wait until they had the money first, before they started dreaming. Big huge mistake! They were probably going to have a long wait!

Eventually they gave up thinking about it and just settled for a much cheaper car. But the real problem wasn't money, it was their thinking. If they got their thinking right, they could create wealth. If you think you can, you can, but if you think you can't, you're right too! The other problem was that they had their thinking backwards, because you don't reduce your dreams to the size of your income level, you dream big and then work on increasing your income to the size of your dreams! In order to do that, you have to believe it is possible! Otherwise you won't bother. Do you believe you will achieve yours? Do you know what they are? Are they written down? I hope so!

Anyway, this person had limited themselves by telling

themselves that they couldn't afford it. So the chances are, they probably never would be able to afford it. After all, that was the command they gave their subconscious. The only way their subconscious would start to work in their favour, was if they changed their words and their beliefs. They were so concerned with the 'how to' that instead of being possibility thinkers, they became 'impossibility thinkers'. Their inner voice would have been "I can't afford it" instead of "I'll find a way to afford it"

I'm sure you've probably met people like that haven't you? I mean people who look for reasons why something can't be done, rather than find reasons why it 'can' be done? Some people continually look for reasons why something won't work. These people are usually experts at complicating the simple, creating problems when there aren't any, and if there are no roadblocks, they create them! But a genius is someone who not only finds solutions, but can take the complex and make it simple. It's all in your perspective. How you see it, is how it will be!

WHATEVER YOU FOCUS ON EXPANDS

Did you know that whatever you focus on, you get more of? Now that's exciting news if you're focusing on good things, but not so exciting if you're focusing on negative things. If you focus on wealth, speak words of prosperity, and create 'wealth habits' such as giving and saving, you will create even more wealth because you are focusing on it. But if you are focusing on poverty, and speaking words of poverty, such as "I can't afford it" and practicing poverty habits, such as greed and getting into debt, then you will create even more poverty because that is also your focus. Your focus becomes one of shortage, and you create even more shortage. So if you aren't earning enough, instead of focusing on your present income level, you need to focus on what you do want to earn. Write it down and do it now!

If you are earning £500 a week, and you need to be earning £5000 per week, don't focus on the fact that you are only earning £500 a week because you are focusing on the problem (shortage) and you will continue to get more of that. Instead, focus on the solution, which is earning £5000 a week (what you want) then you will begin to attract that.

If you are focusing on achieving your dreams, there's a high chance you will achieve them. But if you are focusing on being average and focusing on reasons why you can't achieve your dreams, then you will probably remain average, and never achieve your dreams. Your focus is your choice. Your habits and your actions are your choice, but you can change your focus any time, by changing your actions. What you do daily, will become your focus. Therefore no-one but is responsible for the results in your life but you! You need to be very careful about what you focus on, because you're going to get it! What do you focus on the most? Success or failure? Your dreams or what's on TV? Your dreams or the latest gossip? Your dreams or the latest negative events in the newspapers? Think about someone you know, who continually watches TV and reads newspapers. What's their focus? What do they continually talk about? And how close are they to achieving their dreams? Do they have any? Probably not. Remember, what you focus on, you get more of. If you don't like what you're getting, change your focus, by changing your actions.

When American actress Whoopi Goldberg was asked the secret of her success, she replied "I dreamed about it my whole life" Therefore it's not surprising that she became a success, because that was continually her focus. You will probably find that most high achievers say the same thing. They are very select in what they allow to influence them mentally. And so they should be, because the six inches between our ears is the most valuable piece of real estate any of us will ever have. Ralph Waldo Emerson said "A man is what he thinks about all day long" The Bible says that "As a man thinks in his heart, so is he" (see Prov 23: 7) NKJV

YOUR LEVEL OF BELIEF

How much do you believe you are worth? I don't mean that

literally, but what level of income do you believe you deserve? Do you have a certain amount in your head that you don't feel you can rise above? If that's true, then you need to get rid of that belief right now, or you never will rise above it. Even if you did rise above that income level, your subconscious would quickly recognise that you are out of your comfort zone and pull you back down financially. Subconsciously you would do things to sabotage your own success because you don't believe you deserve all that - unless you change your beliefs.

If you believe that you have a financial ceiling, then as long as you have believed that, your subconscious will have been responding all those years, by keeping you broke. Unless you get rid of it, your subconscious will continue to keep you broke. If you want financial freedom, first of all figure out what financial freedom means to you, in terms of a specific amount. For example, financial freedom to one person might be £50,000 a year, but to another, it might be £100,000 or £500,000. But whatever it is, write it down. And if it helps, you might even want to affirm "I am now making £.................. a year" (fill in your own amount)

This will help to destroy any negative and limiting beliefs you have about your earning capability. The more you say it, the more you will start to replace the old negative beliefs with the new. Then your subconscious will be working for you, instead of against you. Beliefs are never gotten rid of, they are only replaced by new beliefs.

It reminds me of the story of the salesman who could never rise above a certain level of income. The problem was that mentally he had set a limit for himself, and didn't think he was worth any more than that. Neither did he think he was capable of earning a higher level of income. This sent a very definite and powerful message to his subconscious, that he should always earn a certain amount. No more, no less. And of course, his subconscious responded by making sure that he never did make any more than that. But it wasn't an income problem, it was a belief problem.

What have you told yourself about your dreams? Do you believe you'll achieve them, or do you doubt it? Whatever your answer is, remember that your subconscious is working on it day and night, to make it a reality! If you think the odds are against you, they are! If you think the odds are in your favour, they are! If you doubt your dreams will come true, you're right! If you believe they 'can' come true, you're right too! If you believe you have limits, you're right! And you will see limits everywhere. But if you believe you have no limits, you're right too, and you will live an unlimited life. Whatever you tell yourself, good or bad, true or false, will eventually manifest itself in actual physical reality!

DEALING WITH ADVERSITY

Don't think that the road to your dreams is smooth, painless or hassle free, because it certainly isn't. If anyone has told you otherwise, they either don't know what success is, or they're lying! If you want to achieve your dreams, don't think you can achieve them in your present condition. You're going to have to change! You're going to have to deal with fear, disappointment and all kinds of negative emotions. You're going to have to work hard, learn new skills and get rid of old destructive habits. You're also going to have to overcome certain things. And I'm sorry if this sounds a bit blunt, but the main thing you're going to have to overcome is yourself. I can say that from experience, because I now have a completely different way of thinking, use different words, have a different attitude, and a different way of looking at life. I also have a renewed faith in God that I never had before. I am also far happier than I was before. I can honestly tell you that every ounce of pain, every negative emotion, every tear and every bit of rejection, every bit of ridicule, every bit of hard work, every bit of sacrifice and every bit of sweat is ABSOLUTELY WORTH IT!!

I can only speak from my own point of view, but of all the rewards I have experienced, since I first started out many years ago, is my relationship with the Lord Jesus Christ. I'm not saying that will be the same for you. I am only telling you about me. But I would not be where I am just now without Him. Often when I was going through my toughest times, He would pick me up, just when I wanted to give up. When I was confused, He would make things clear, and explain them to me. But one thing I want to make absolutely clear is this; God did not allow me to avoid pain. Instead He helped me 'in' my pain. God does not prevent hardship and suffering, even to His own followers, instead He helps you 'through it'. In order to receive His help, you need to ask Him. You need to include Him in your life. The reason I am talking about all this is because even although you are pursuing your dreams, it's not all going to be plain sailing. Yes, there will be a lot of fun times ahead. Yes, there will be good times, and you will meet some interesting people, but there are also going to be tough times, and times when you feel like giving up. That's when you also need to focus on your dream.

American business guru Dexter Yager is famous for saying "When your dream is big enough, the facts don't count" because when your dream is big enough, you will still be focusing on your dream. But if your dream is too small, you won't be able to see it for adversity. It doesn't matter what fears you have, it could be a fear of public speaking, it could be a fear of dealing with people, it could be a fear of anything, but if your dream is bigger than your fear, nothing will stop you. It might not be fear that is your biggest obstacle. Maybe you hate rejection and you feel like giving up. Maybe people keep disappointing you and letting you down. Maybe they keep wasting your time and you feel like you're getting nowhere fast. Maybe you're putting in maximum effort and nothing's happening. Don't be surprised if this happens! At some point, it happens to most successful people. However, it doesn't last forever. Eventually you get through it, and things turn around, as long as you persist. When your dreams are big enough, psychologically it will look like this:

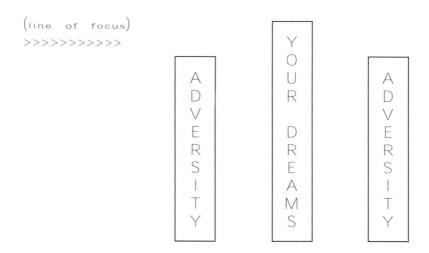

When your dreams are big enough, you will still be able to focus on them, in the midst of adversity. You need to find a dream so big that it takes your breath away. It needs to be something so big that you can't possibly achieve it with your current level of income. Then when adversity strikes, you've got a reason to keep going. When someone laughs at you and tells you, you can't do it, you've got a reason to get out there and do it! When you get a hundred rejections in a row, you've got a reason to keep going!

However, if your dreams are too small, and your fears are bigger than your dreams, you usually quit. You simply lose sight of your dreams and tell yourself it just isn't worth it, to go through all the heartbreak and pain. Psychologically it will look like this:

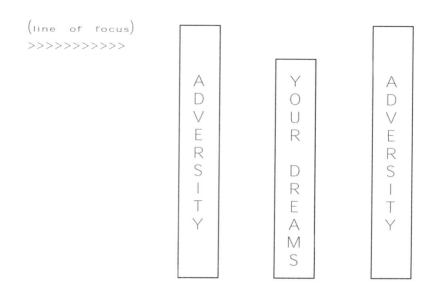

(line of focus)
>>>>>>>>>>>

Most people I know who quit the MLM business did so when they were going through a tough time. Obviously their dreams were too small, or they would have kept going. But a dream **doesn't have to be a selfish dream. Neither does it have to be** something material. For example, maybe your dream is to raise millions of pounds for cancer research? You certainly **can't** do it just now, working your day job, so you need to step out of your comfort zone and do something different.

MOMENTUM

If you want to achieve your dreams, you need to have momentum. But what exactly is momentum? In physics, we are told momentum = mass x velocity. Which means that the bigger the mass of an object and the higher its velocity, the more unstoppable it becomes? Imagine a car parked at the top of a hill. The owner has accidentally left the handbrake off, and it starts to roll **down the hill. At first it doesn't have much momentum as it** very slowly starts to move. But wait a minute or so, and it will be virtually unstoppable, because of its increased velocity and momentum.

In the same way, we can gain momentum and become virtually unstoppable, if we choose to put some effort in. But to get to that point, we have to start. It reminds me of the story of a group of men trying to shove a huge truck. These men were struggling to try and push it. People standing at the side of the road were saying to each other "They'll never get it moving". Eventually the wheels of the truck slowly began to turn. Gradually it began to gain speed. As its speed increased, it required less and less effort to keep it going. Soon it had so much momentum that it looked as though nothing could stop it. The people at the side of the road now said "They'll never get it stopped" The ironic thing was, that they were talking about the exact same object. The only difference was that it had momentum.

Do you have momentum? The way to tell if you have momentum or not, is by what you do every day. Do you do something every day, towards the achievement of your dreams? It might be a phone call. It might be doing some dream building, or showing a presentation. Or it might simply be reading from a self help book every day. All of these things put together, help to create momentum. The more you do the more momentum you have. Also, the busier you are, the less chance of quitting. Why? Let me use an example; If you have one presentation a week and the person says "No", it's a really big deal, because you have the rest of the week to focus on the "No" (focusing on the problem) But if you have four or five presentations a week and one of them says "No", you are so busy thinking about your next appointment (focusing on the solution) that you don't have time to focus on the "No". You also know that you still have three or four potential "Yes-es", so it doesn't bother you half as much. That's the beauty of momentum. Keep it going and it will be easier to keep going. Believe it or not, but the biggest threat to your momentum are two main things; when things are going well and when things are going badly. Why? Because when things are going well, we often think we've got it made, and start to coast. We start to take it easy. Often, this is when we can lose momentum; we start to live on successes of the past, rather than live in the present moment and keep the momentum going. When things are going badly, we often get so discouraged that we take a break. The Bible warns against this in the book of Proverbs ; "A little sleep, a little slumber, a little folding of the hands to rest - and poverty will come on you like a bandit and scarcity like an armed man" (Prov 6: 10-11). Unfortunately, some people give up completely. They may start again a while later, but by that time, they've lost momentum. It's just like pushing a big truck; they had it moving, but now it's at a complete standstill and they have to start all over again. It's much harder to start from a complete standstill, than to push something which is already moving. So, keep the momentum going, and never slack off, whether you're going through good times or bad! The ironic thing is that things will always be either good or bad -- they can't be anything else, can they? I must admit that this is hard to do, because we are only human. But it can be done! The secret to keeping your momentum is by focusing on your dream, no matter what is happening. If something goes wrong, focus on your dream! If someone lets you down, focus on your dream! If someone says your idea will never work, focus on your dream! If someone says "You're not capable", focus on your dream! If someone says "I'm not interested", focus on your dream! If you find you're burning the candle at both ends, focus on your dream! If you're putting in maximum effort, and getting nowhere, focus on your dream! If you collapse into your bed at the end of the night because you've been working so hard, focus on your wife! You get the point, don't you? Adversity happens, but the key is not to focus on it!

NEVER GIVE UP!

Remember the words of Winston Churchill; "Never, never, never, never, give up! If you want to achieve your dreams, you need to develop the "Never say die" attitude. You need to refuse to surrender, no matter what. Its only people with this attitude that make it! Because of Churchill's defiance and positive attitude, he inspired a nation, when Great Britain was on its knees.

Andy Holligan

At this particular time, invasion was imminent and the whole world was sure that Britain would fall to the Nazi's. But Churchill informed Hitler that Great Britain would fight to the last man, and the rest is history.

> "We shall go on to the end, we shall fight in France, we shall fight on the seas and oceans, we shall fight with growing confidence and growing strength in the air, we shall defend our island, whatever the cost may be, we shall fight on the beaches, we shall fight on the landing grounds, we shall fight in the fields and in the streets, we shall fight in the hills, we shall never surrender!"
>
> (Sir Winston Churchill)
> June 4, 1940
> House of Commons

CHAPTER 9

GIVING BACK

"Whoever trusts in his riches will fall, but the righteous will thrive like a green leaf" (Prov 11: 28)

We must never get to a point where we are so focused on our dreams and ambitions that we forget about helping other people. True happiness is found in the giving, not in the taking. There's nothing wrong with ambition or becoming wealthy, but we must have a higher purpose than ourselves, otherwise there will be emptiness in our lives. In my opinion, helping other people financially should be equally important as our own dreams and desires. This might seem to contradict what I've just said in the previous chapter, but it doesn't. There is no limit to what we can achieve, if we are using it for good purposes. Achieving our dreams should be a win-win situation. The more successful we become, the more we should be doing to help people less fortunate than ourselves. As our financial situation improves, so should our giving increase. If we have trebled our income, then our giving should at least have trebled. The more successful we become, the more God demands from us. The Bible says "From everyone who has been given much, much will be demanded ; and from the one who has been entrusted with much, much more will be asked" (Luke 12: 48)

Does this mean it's wrong to become wealthy, or to set a goal to own a luxury car or own a big mansion in the country? No, not at all, but it depends on the person. Let me explain; one person (Mr A) might set a goal to own a new car. Perhaps he has achieved it, but doesn't give a second thought to giving anything to the poor because he is so absorbed in his own desires. He might have trebled his income in order to buy the new car, but still don't give anything to the poor. While another person (Mr B) in the exact same financial situation might also have achieved the same car, but contribute a significant part of his income to the poor. Mr 'B' has also trebled his income, and chooses to give three times as much to charity as he did before. Thus, he has created a win-win situation. More people are now benefiting because of Mr 'B's success. If he hadn't achieved it, then he wouldn't be able to help as many people. But Mr 'A's desire was purely selfish, and no-one else benefited, as a result of his success. This is what God condemns! He doesn't condemn the money or the car, He condemns the person.

Remember that the Bible doesn't condemn ambition, it only condemns selfish ambition. "Do nothing out of selfish ambition or vain conceit, but in humility consider others better than you. Each of you should look not only to your own interests, but also to the interests of others (Phil 2: 3-4)

Those two people might have had the exact same goal to achieve the exact same car, achieved the same level of income, but their choices and priorities were different. Can you see how it is not money or material possessions that are wrong, but it is people who are right or wrong because of their attitudes and the choices they make? Money and material possessions are simply objects. Only when we get so wrapped up in our own desires that we forget about helping others, does it become wrong. But there has to be something in it for us too, or we would never be motivated to do the work. That's why you need to dream, and dream big! The bigger your dream, the more people you can help.

Never let anyone tell you that money is evil, or that it is the root of all evil because that is one of the most misquoted verses in the Bible. This attitude will also keep you broke and stop you from achieving. The truth is, the Bible actually condemns peoples 'attitude towards money' and not the actual money itself. It says "For the love of money is a root of all kinds of evil" (1 Tim 6: 10) If you let money become the number one thing in your life, it is a sin. Money has now taken the place of God, and money becomes your god. If you manipulate people or exploit them in order to make more money, it is a sin. Money has now become more important than people, which is also a form of idolatry. Money should always be kept in its proper perspective. Once that happens, and you start doing the right things, you will find that money comes more easily and readily to you.

There was the story of the man walking along the road when a charity worker approached him and asked if he could spare some change for the poor. He replied "Help the poor? I can't even help myself!" Obviously this man had his thinking backwards, because he was waiting until his financial situation improved, 'before' he was willing to give. Not only is this wrong, but his financial situation will never improve with this type of thinking, for it is the very act of giving that causes our financial situation to improve in the first place. The way to wealth is by being generous, not by being stingy. The Bible says "A generous man will prosper. He who refreshes others will himself be refreshed" (Prov 11: 25)

The Devil wants us to believe that being greedy will cause us to end up with more. This is not only extremely deceptive, but also a huge lie. Proverbs tells us "A stingy man is eager to get rich and is unaware that poverty awaits him" (Prov 28: 22). The reason it is so deceptive is because from a logical point of view, it would seem to make sense. Worldly thinking tells us that greed equals more, but in reality, greed causes lack and shortage. Greed is like a boomerang; it always comes back on you. Many of God's principles seem to go against logic, which instead, requires us to have faith. For example we might not understand how it can be possible to give, and end up with more. But the bottom line is this; if we don't have the faith, then we are not going to see the results or reap the rewards. But if we choose to put our faith in God and trust His principles, we will prosper. This principle of giving, totally opposes what the Devil is trying to get us to believe. Giving is the way to wealth! Not that we should give 'to get' but that's how it works.

THE EYE OF THE NEEDLE

When I first became involved in the MLM business and everyone was talking about becoming wealthy, I was extremely concerned because of the "eye of the needle" principle. Jesus said to his disciples "I tell you the truth; it is hard for a rich man to enter the kingdom of heaven. Again I tell you, it is easier for a camel to go through the eye of a needle than for a rich man to enter the kingdom of God" When the disciples heard this, they were greatly astonished and asked, "Who then can be saved?" Jesus looked at them and said "With man this is impossible, but with God all things are possible" (Mat 19: 23-26)

I knew that a camel could never fit through the eye of a needle, and I assumed this meant that it was impossible to get into heaven if you were rich. If this was the case, then all rich people would go to hell! I didn't want to go to hell! But I didn't realise that in Biblical times, the eye of the needle was a name given to a narrow gate in a Jerusalem city wall. In those days, the cities had walls to protect them from invading armies. A camel could get through this gate but it was very difficult. It either had to be unloaded or pass through on its knees. Very difficult but not impossible.

Jesus didn't say it was impossible, He said it was difficult. Why? Because of man's tendency to cast God aside. The Bible says "Some people, eager for money, have wandered from the faith and pierced themselves with many grief's" (1 Tim 6: 10) Some people get so absorbed in making money that it becomes their god, and they feel they don't need God in their lives. When money becomes the central thing in your life, you are not happy. Apart from squeezing God out of the picture, you end up suffering from greed. Remember that greed is a negative emotion, and cannot co-exist with happiness. Therefore, greedy people are not happy. The Bible also says "People who want to get rich fall into temptation and a trap and into many foolish and harmful desires that plunge men into ruin and destruction" (1 Tim 6: 9)

How many times have we heard of pop stars or famous people getting involved in drugs or promiscuous behaviour? How many famous people do we hear about, getting involved in sexually immoral behaviour? Quite a few! But you don't have to be famous, this warning applies to 'any' rich person, famous or not! Yes, the Bible gives many warnings to the rich and people who want to get rich, but it also tells us that God wants us to prosper. In my opinion, people who believe it is wrong to be rich, have failed to consider other verses in the Bible. We should always take into account what other Bible verses say too. We should always compare scripture with other parts of scripture, before making an overall informed decision.

The Bible makes it clear that wealth is part of our reward for obedience to God. In other words, if we fully obey Him, and put Him at the centre of our lives, then wealth and all kinds of blessings, including material blessings, will come upon us. Deuteronomy chapter 30 talks about "Prosperity after turning to the Lord". The Book of Proverbs says "With me are riches and honour, enduring wealth and prosperity" (Prov 8: 18) The Bible also talks about "Bestowing wealth on those who love me and making their treasuries full" (Prov 8: 21)

Therefore, being rich in and of itself is not a sin. It depends on the person and how they think towards riches. It also depends how they live their lives, and what they do with their money. Did they gain the money honestly or not? Do they do good with their money or are they greedy? Do they love money or do they love God? Is money their master or is God their Master? What are their priorities? Is money number one, or is God number One? Do they put people before money, or do they put money before people? We all need to ask ourselves these questions, and be brutally honest with ourselves, otherwise we are fooling ourselves. We may fool ourselves, and we might even fool other people, but we cannot fool God. "For the Lord searches every heart and understands every motive behind the thoughts" (1 Chron 28: 9)

THE WEALTH OF NATION, DEPENDS ON THE WEALTH OF ITS PEOPLE

We must remember that if there were no rich, then the country would be in a sorry state. We need the rich to provide goods and services. We need business owners to provide jobs. We need people to provide housing. We need banks to lend us money. We need investors to pour money into the country. We also need people to spend money. If we didn't have people spending money, our economy would suffer. For example, if people stopped buying fancy cars, there would be lay-offs because the people who produce these things would be out of work, for lack of demand. The people, who are now out of work, would also have less money to spend because they are unemployed. This, in turn, would have a knock-on effect on the rest of the economy. And on it goes. So society needs people to spend money. Therefore, wealthy is healthy!

HOW MUCH SHOULD WE GIVE?

I've heard people saying "You should give until it hurts" But in my opinion, that is a cop-out answer. Why? Because it's too vague. It is not specific enough. Not only that, but it implies that giving is something to be dreaded, or grudged. The Bible says "Each man should give what he has decided in his heart to give, not reluctantly or under compulsion, for God loves a cheerful giver" (2 Cor 9: 7)

If we talk about giving until it hurts, a person might give two percent of their income and say that it hurts. Another might give nothing, and only give when there is an appeal for a disaster, or some kind of international crisis. They might also claim that it hurts. But who is to say what hurts? No-one can really define what hurts. That's why God tells us very specifically, to give a certain amount. The amount is a tenth. The Bible refers to this as 'Tithing' (tithe- meaning 'tenth') God tells us that if we give a tenth of everything, we will have abundance. "Bring the whole tithe into the storehouse, that there may be food in my house. Test me in this says the Lord Almighty, and see if I will not throw open the floodgates of heaven and pour out so much blessing that you will not have room enough for it" (Mal 3 : 8-10)

Think about it, who could grudge giving when you see pictures of babies in Africa starving to death? As soon as they're born, they're dying. Who could grudge giving when people have to walk miles for water and we only have to turn on a tap! Does it not make you want to give all you can? Giving should never hurt! Giving is something we should want to do! For it is only by the grace of God that we have what we have. Things could easily be the other way about!

One day God is going to ask us what we did with our lives. He might say "Why should I let you in my heaven? Is the world a better place, for you having lived? What good did you do ME? And do you know what your response will be? Because that day will come! When we get to that point, we might wish we had done more, but it will be too late! But it's not too late yet! The time is NOW!

EVERYTHING COUNTS

Consider the case of Fred. Fred gets a letter through the door appealing for donations for cancer research. In the letter, it asks if he would consider setting up a direct debit for £2 a month. But Fred thinks to himself "£2 a month? What difference will that make?" and throws it in the bin. But let's say that every household in Britain gets one of those letters, and we estimate the population at around 60 million- just for a round figure. That's potentially, a lot of donations. How many people will have the same attitude as Fred? Sure there will be a lot of people who agree, but just to take it to the extreme, let's suppose that everyone has the same attitude as Fred. What does cancer research receive in donations? £0

Now let's suppose that everyone in Britain agrees to give just £2 a month. How much does cancer research receive in donations then? In my estimation, 60 million x £2 = £120 million. Is there much difference between £0 and £120 million? You bet! Cancer research now receives £120 million instead of nothing, all because people changed their attitudes. Instead of thinking "What difference will £2 a month make?" they thought "It may not be much individually, but collectively, it can make a massive difference" As a result, more progress is made towards cancer research. Remember, God doesn't expect you to bear the burdens of the whole world on your shoulders. He expects everyone else to do their part too, whether rich, poor or middle class. If you give, and other people don't, that's their problem. Don't worry about it. You are only responsible for doing your part, and each individual will have to, one day give account of themselves before God. (See Rom 14: 12)

There seems to be a belief among some people that it is wrong to be rich, and there is something holy about being poor. In my opinion, there are good and bad people at both ends of the spectrum. There are good and bad rich people, and there are good and bad poor people. Money has nothing to do with it. A lot of people always try and bring money into the equation, to determine whether someone is good or bad. Not that we should be judging people, but many people do. There are some very generous rich people and there are some greedy rich people. There are some very kind and pleasant poor people, who would give you their last piece of bread, but there are also a lot of criminals who come from poor backgrounds. Money is not a factor, in determining whether someone is good or bad. But ultimately we will be judged by God for our actions and our attitudes towards money and towards other people.

"Then the King will say to those on his right, 'Come, you who are blessed by my Father; take your inheritance, the kingdom prepared for you since the creation of the world. For I was hungry and you gave me something to eat, I was thirsty and you gave me something to drink, I was a stranger and you invited me in, I needed clothes and you clothed me, I was sick and you looked after me, I was in prison and you came to visit me'.

Then the righteous will answer him, Lord, when did we see you hungry and feed you, or thirsty and give you something to drink? When did we see you a stranger and invite you in, or needing clothes and clothe you? When did we see you sick or in prison and go to visit you?'

The King will reply, 'I tell you the truth, whatever you did for one of the least of these brothers of mine, you did for me. (Mat 25: 34 - 40)

May God bless you in your quest for success. Keep reading, keep believing, keep dreaming and never, never, never, never give up!

About The Author

Andy Holligan is an independent business owner in his native Scotland, Great Britain. He became involved in multi level marketing in 1995, which he worked part-time. The sales and training system changed his life- way beyond his expectations and he became a Christian in 1999.

What Holligan has written about in his books is based not on 'classroom theory', but on his own personal experience over a period of years. His hope is that other people might avoid the pitfalls he fell into and at the same time, benefit from what he has experienced. Please visit his website at:

www.solutionstoyourlife.com

Other titles by the same author:

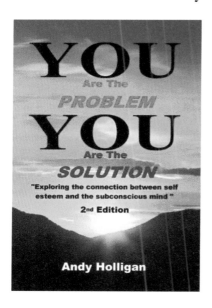

ISBN 978-1-911090-87-8

BV - #0023 - 030620 - C0 - 229/152/14 - PB - 9781911090878